A Roads Scholar

An Anecdotal Account of One Man's Life on the Road

Ivan E. Young

Order this book online at www.trafford.com
or email orders@trafford.com

Most Trafford titles are also available at major online book retailers.

Printed in the United States of America.

ISBN: 978-1-4120-1822-7 (sc)

Trafford rev. 06/26/2014

Trafford
PUBLISHING® www.trafford.com
North America & international
toll-free: 1 888 232 4444 (USA & Canada)
fax: 812 355 4082

ACKNOWLEDGEMENTS

When I set out to relate the story of my life, I found that I had to touch on the lives of many people. Without the material that they unwittingly supplied, I would not have been able to write this documentary.

Special mention goes to my wife, Sue, who has endured me for so many years and has assisted me in the production of this story, providing me with her own memories of our life together. She was also a major help in the editing of the story.

I thank my daughter, Pam, who came up with the idea in the first place and my son, Bryan, for his assistance in the proofreading along with Judith Maxwell

Special mention goes to June Carr for her help through several revisions to the final editing, and to Angie Boland for her contribution to the graphic layout.

Thanks to all whose escapades appear on these pages. I have used discretion, and sometimes changed the names to protect the guilty. Any disparaging reference to any person alive or deceased is unintentional. To all I am forever grateful.

INTRODUCTION

The following stories have been out of memory for so many years that minor errors may occur. However, each episode is based on truth but may be, at times, spiced up to prevent boredom.

Dizzy Dean once said. "It ain't braggin' if you done it." That was okay for Dizzy to say. As you read this documentary you may think, with good reason, that some of the escapades don't fall into the category of "bragging material."

In the area of Ontario around Georgian Bay, Grey County sprawls in an expanse encompassing the Blue Mountains and is bordered on the north by Georgian Bay.

The principal rivers in Grey County are the Beaver, the Saugeen, the Mad, and the Sauble. The county is also endowed with numerous lakes. The main industry, as in any other rural area, is farming. Many areas of Grey County are remote and difficult to access.

The Third Line of Osprey Township in the "dirty thirties" was about as remote as it gets. It was on the Third Line in nineteen thirty-two that I was born—Ivan Earl Young—on a stormy December day.

Perhaps the fact that my life has, on occasion, had its stormy times can be attributed to the stormy day of my birth. Or was it because I landed on Planet Earth on the thirteenth? Whatever the case may be, I have had my share of fair weather and I am happy to relate my experiences and escapades here to the best of my ability. As the story unfolds we go from the Great Depression into World War Two and sixty years of change like the world has never known. We have gone from the days of the horse and plow of the thirties to the days of landing men on the moon. We moved to the computer age. All this was accomplished before the millennium year.

Come travel with me on this sometimes rocky, often humorous voyage through my life from the Great Depression to the Twenty First Century.

GROWING UP

Osprey Township in the County of Grey was, and still is, noted for its stormy winters with lots of snow and cold.

December 13, 1932 was no exception. That is the day I was born to Nellie and Wesley Young in the big brick house on the Young homestead, on

The Young Homestead Where I was born.

the Third Line of Osprey Township. I was the first born of an eventual family of five boys. In 1932 the world was in the depths of the Great Depression, so Mom and Dad lived with his parents. There were no jobs and no money so we lived at the homestead until a second son was born. He was named Clarence.

Near my Grandfather's farm Grandfather had "rented" a pasture farm. I say rented although I don't believe he paid a nickel in rent because the owner had left years before and no one knew or cared where he was. It had belonged to a Mr. Spencer who abandoned it in 1930 because he couldn't make a living. Rumour had it that he lost the place to the government because he was unable to pay twenty dollars in back taxes. This was a prime example of the hardships and broken dreams caused by the Great Depression.

On the farm there was a log house that was built in the 1800's by a Mr. Winters and his wife, Rebecca. At the time it was built, the area was wilderness with Indian settlements all around. When Mr. Winters died, Becky remained there alone.

There is a large marsh to the south of the log cabin. Blueberries or huckleberries grew in the marsh and the local pioneers would pick them in season. The marsh was so dense that occasionally a berry picker would get lost and never be seen again. This strange tract of land became known as the Mystery Marsh.

Becky had a sister who lived on the other side of the marsh, about five miles south. A trail led through the marsh and Becky walked this trail whenever she made one of her occasional visits to see her sister.

It was presumed that Becky made one last trip to her sister's place, but she didn't arrive. She disappeared without a trace. There are strange stories told even today of the Mystery Marsh.

The old log house laid empty for many years until Mr. Spencer moved in around 1920 and tried to make a living by farming. He lost the farm about 1930, in the middle of the depression and the old house was again vacant.

About this time my mother and father had enough of living in someone else's house. They were young and ambitious and decided to make the log house livable again. At least they would have a home of their own.

They fixed the windows and put doors on the house. As I remember, the first doors had leather hinges. They found an old cook-stove and hooked it up to the chimney. Dad was a handyman of sorts and made some of the furniture and cupboards. Actually the kitchen cupboards were just three shelves on the wall, with a curtain hung in front.

There was a little table by the cupboard shelves and it served as a counter. A pail of water from the well sat on this table and a tin dipper was used to dip the water. A washbasin sat on the table as well. On cold winter mornings we had to break the ice in the water pail.

Dad usually got up and got the wood fire going and the old log house would warm up in no time. The house had a good-sized living room with two rooms adjacent. One was a bedroom large enough for a bed, a dresser and a baby's crib—because by now there was a third son, Raymond.

The other room was really more like a closet. It was six feet by six feet, and had no windows. It became the bedroom for Clarence and myself.

Dad had no work because Canada was still in the depths of the Great Depression so he decided to capitalize on his skills. He built a workbench in the kitchen along the south wall under the window. The kitchen cupboards were on the north wall, so with the cook stove, the homemade kitchen table, and some benches to sit on, we had a busy kitchen.

6

Now Dad had his workbench and was ready to begin his work. His tools were so old they could well have been used in Egypt to build the pyramids. His Dad gave him an old hammer, he found a drawknife in a junk pile, and in time he accumulated an assortment of rusty chisels, a screwdriver and numerous other gadgets that were no longer of use to anyone else.

It was amazing how much my father could accomplish with so few tools. He was frugal with what little money he had, which is why he had no tools. In his "workshop", he made axe handles and sold them to the neighbours. Everyone had a woodpile in those days.

He made a violin with little more than a jack-knife. A professional fiddler in Toronto used it for a number of years. I have the fiddle in my possession now and it is a masterpiece considering the primitive tools with which he crafted it.

In the summer of 1935 there was still no letup in the depression, so he built a buzz saw and sawed firewood for the farmers. He found a set of sheep shears somewhere so he got into the wool shearing business, and was paid ten cents a sheep to shear them.

A Steam engine model built by Father. It has all working parts. He built it with the crudest of tools.

By now his family had grown to four sons with the arrival of Carl and he had to work hard to provide for us.

My Dad was never much of an entrepreneur and he had to do everything the hard way.

Another of my father's endeavours was his first truck, which he actually built. It had a Reo cab and radiator, a Chevrolet engine and I believe the transmission and rear end were from a Pierce Arrow car. It had hard rubber tires and a box about six feet by six feet.

Once he decided to take a load of wood to Dundalk, which was a distance of ten miles. A load of wood on that truck was equal to about three wheelbarrow loads and he could reach supersonic speeds of ten MPH. A neighbour went with him and joked that he should walk on ahead and get things ready to unload the wood.

They all laughed at "Wes and his truck" but it was the start of his life in the transport business.

Somewhere around this time son number five arrived. He was named Stanley.

This completed our family and the old house was starting to bulge at the seams, but it was our home and many good times were had in the log house.

One of the few pictures of the Log House
L-to-R Carl and Stanley

In the winter of 1936 I became very ill. We had no phone as phones were just coming in, so Dad went to a neighbour's and phoned the doctor in Dundalk.

The doctor came to the house by horse and sleigh and after he looked me over they rushed me to Markdale Hospital, a distance of about 15 miles, in the doctor's horse and sleigh. My appendix had been burst for longer than they realized. The doctor gave me little or no hope, but mother wouldn't give up.

She stayed in the room with me the whole time. I went from the hospital to a convalescing home in Markdale. They wanted me close to a doctor for a few days yet.

Finally I was allowed to go home to the log house, happy to be home. "Be it ever so humble, there is no place like home."

We had many good times in the log house, and we were living evidence to the fact that you don't have to have money to have a good time.

A LOG HOUSE CHRISTMAS

We used to go to the swamp at the back of the farm and cut a spruce tree and drag it home for Christmas. We would stand it in the corner of the main room and adorn it with our own homemade decorations. We made popcorn strings and paper chains and other things, using whatever we found around the house; such as old Christmas cards, last year's wrapping paper etc. All in all it cost nothing because that's how much we had to spend.

Mother would put us to bed at night, and then using Dad's workbench and his primitive tools she made us little wooden toy cars. The wheels were cut from a broomstick. She painted them pretty colours and put them under the tree on Christmas Eve when we were all in bed. In the morning we would all be up at or before daylight. It was frigid in the morning in that old house but we didn't care, we were too excited about Christmas.

One year father built a beautiful sled. It was shared by all of us. In our family we learned to share very young.

I remember one Christmas when we all got up at the crack of dawn and headed for the tree. There stood a beautiful bright red tricycle. It was all steel, quite unlike the wooden homemade toys we were used to. But steel has it bad points, especially on a cold winter morning when the temperature is about 10 below freezing.

Clarence immediately found one of the bad points of a steel seat. His two-piece pyjamas had fallen down exposing his derriere. He jumped on the tricycle and stuck fast to the seat! We got warm water out of the reservoir on the stove and finally got him free.

After the gift giving was over and the commotion settled down we would have a breakfast of porridge. I hated porridge, but on Christmas day I ate it all up.

Christmas always had a religious ring to it because my grandparents were ardent churchgoers. Grandmother was a religious fanatic.

About ten o'clock Christmas morning we could hear the sleigh bells ringing as Grandpa drove up in the sleigh to take us to his house for Christmas dinner, which was only about 15 minutes away by horse and sleigh.

It was a joy to hear the sleigh bells and the sound of everyone singing carols.

When we arrived we greeted all our cousins who were already there. The whole lot numbered about fifteen kids. There would be carol singing as we stood around the organ in the parlour, but the kids were usually too excited about Christmas to sing carols for any length of time. We would all show off our gifts from Santa, although none of us believed in Santa too seriously.

There were always board games to play; crokinole was probably the most popular.

For the more rowdy ones there was a sled or two outside and lots of things to do in Grandfathers barn, in the hayloft, climbing on the beams and jumping onto the hay. Some of us got our kicks out of poking the horses with sticks to make them jump.

Grandfather had two older horses—Barney, a big Sorrel with an almost white mane and tail, a handsome animal; and Kate, a big, Bay Clydesdale mare. They were a fine team and Grandfather was proud of them, but Barney had a problem. He had the heaves.

Have you ever seen a horse with the heaves? Make that have you HEARD a horse with the heaves? Barney would let go with a tremendous cough and the strain would make him fire at the rear as well. When Barney let one of his double-ended coughs go, it made the barn doors rattle. Good old Barney!

We then sat down to Christmas dinner and after Grandmother gave a rather dragged out blessing, we all got started. What a feast—roast goose with all the trimmings—and Christmas pudding for dessert. It sure was a change from the usual meal we got in the dirty thirties.

We thought winters were great and two or three weeks after New Years my brothers and I would go back to the swamp to drag another tree home. We would decorate it up and have Christmas all over again. I don't know how Mother kept her sanity sometimes.

THE ULTIMATE BAD DAY

We would have some especially bad days, one I remember quite well. It was springtime and Mother was getting the garden ready to plant. She had arranged the packages of seeds on the kitchen table.

Kids have an impulse to do the things that their parents do, and we were no exception. Mother was planting a garden, so why couldn't we plant a garden?

Later on Mother came in to get her seeds and not one package was left on the table. She rounded us up and it didn't take a genius to sense trouble. She questioned (well, actually, interrogated) each of us about the seeds and mentioned the dire consequences if we didn't tell her where the seeds were. Not one of us said a word.

I must say we kids sure stuck together.

A couple of weeks later Mother made a discovery.

The old dug well had good moist soil around it from all the water being spilled and we found it very easy to dig a hole in this soil, which we did and dumped a whole pack of seeds in each hole. They started to come through the ground in clumps—a clump of radishes here, a clump of lettuce there, etc.

Later that very same day Mother happened to glance up. She couldn't believe her eyes. All five of us were lined up on the ridge top of the house including Stan who was about two years old. Mother got us down from there very carefully. After she got us on good old "terra firma," we got a rather blunt lesson about our status in life. We were told in no uncertain terms that we were not monkeys and shouldn't behave like monkeys.

The older ones were designated the instigators and received the appropriate punishment which consisted of some good old whops with Dad's razor strap. We decided to leave home rather than put up with all this abuse. I was six years old at the time, and my brothers were all younger. We went around to the back of the house out of sight and planned our getaway.

Mother decided things were a little too quiet so she came looking for us. We were nowhere to be found. After checking the barn and calling us she began to panic and ran down the long lane to the road just in time to see all five of us, hand in hand, spanning the full width of the road and rounding the corner. We were headed for Grandma's. Surely life would be better and, besides, Grandma didn't use Grandpa's razor strap on the grandchildren.

I don't remember much more about that day. It had been a pretty full day. That night I am sure we slept well.

KABOOM!

Mother spent a lot of time in her garden in the summer. She figured that on a big old farm there should be lots of room for us to run and play without getting into too much trouble. Wrong!

One of those days was a little cooler than usual so we spent some time in the house. On a shelf on top of a window Dad had some gunpowder stored in a pretty tin with a lid on it. He figured it would be safe on that high shelf. Wrong again!

We decided that we wanted that pretty little tin can so by using chairs, the table and some books to stand on we got the tin down. We didn't know what the contents were, nor did we care, we just wanted the tin can. So what do you do when you want to get rid of something? You throw it in the stove. Being a cool day, there was a small fire in the stove. I marched over and opened the door on the front of the stove and threw in the contents of the tin can. There was a terrific KABOOM!!! All the stove lids went flying and a ball of fire came out of the front door of the stove where I was standing. It singed my eyebrows and eyelashes and singed all the hair sticking out of the bottom of the toque I was wearing. I was sure I was headed for the pearly gates that time.

That fall I started school and a whole new chapter in my life was about to begin...

SCHOOL DAZE

Hatherton School House was one-and-a-half miles from our house. On the first day of school my mother had sewn me a new pair of bibbed overalls, made from flour sacks and dyed blue. I was six years old. Clarence went to school too, although he was only five, and he also had a pair of bibbed overalls. The reason for Clarence also being sent to school was because it was such a long walk for me, a six year old. They must have forgotten Clarence was only five.

So we marched off to school all by ourselves with our lunch pails (which were honey pails with wire handles). The trouble was that most of the other kids had honey pails as well so it sometimes ended in mass confusion.

Hatherton was a bright little brick schoolhouse with a nice basement where we played at recess when the weather was bad.

On extremely bad days we stayed home from school. It was fun looking out of the house window at a raging blizzard and knowing that there was no school that day. We were warm and cozy in the little log house.

The school had no water, so there was an outhouse and a well where we got water in a pail for drinking.

I remember one recess in the late fall when I had to go to the bathroom. The big kids had taken control of the outhouse and the little kids were not allowed to use it. I wet my pants! When recess was over I went into the school crying and the teacher, Mr. Ring, asked me what was wrong. I didn't want to tell him the real problem so I showed him a scratch I had on my hand from two or three days before. "Oh," he said "I know how to fix your sore hand, just come over here and stand close to the stove. That should heal it real quick." I'll never forget Mr. Ring. He was a great teacher and a friend.

Shortly after I started public school, our grandfather gave us a dog, mainly because our old dog, Scottie, had lived out his life and Grandfather felt we needed a dog. Prin was a female, about a year old when she came to live at our place in the log house. She was an English Setter, mostly black with a white face and black spots. I guess Prin (a rather odd name) was the beginning of my love affair with dogs.

For some reason she picked me out of our clan and became my dog. Prin turned out to be a very prolific dog and as a result we had puppies around our place a lot of the time. In those days few people had their female dogs spayed. In our case it was mainly because Father wouldn't part with the money, as he didn't have a great love for pets.

MISS COLPAS

When we lived in the log house, a missionary lady sometimes came to the Gordon Farm to visit. Her name was Miss Colpas and she worked among the people of the North. Her main interest was young people, and she had a wonderful way with them.

She held us all rapt by telling stories of her experiences in remote areas using simple language and everybody listened. Another reason we listened was because at the end of one of her meetings everybody received a gift–probably worth about five cents but worth a hundred dollars to a kid.

Every time she came to the Gordon's they held a meeting and kids from all around were invited. The area was sparsely populated so about a dozen kids would show up. The night of Miss Colpas' arrival was always one of the highlights of our year.

WORLD WAR TWO

In 1939 the storm clouds began to gather over Europe. Hitler had occupied Poland and was preparing to invade the Baltic States. The German navy led by the Bismarck was sinking English merchant ships in the north Atlantic.

The British Prime Minister, Neville Chamberlain, finally declared war on Germany in 1939.

Canada was a colony of the British Empire so we were in the war. Australia was also a colony and they came in along with all the other British colonies. This group of countries was called the Allies. So it was the Allies against Germany.

The Great Depression had ravaged the world for close to ten years. Hitler saw this as a time to conquer the world.

To a kid about seven years old this was an exciting time compared to the depression. Thousands of young men joined the armed forces. Sixteen was the minimum age to enlist but many fifteen-year-olds lied about their age and enlisted. To these young men it was a bed to sleep on, food, and the excitement of war. Many of them got more excitement than they bargained for.

Mackenzie King was Prime Minister of Canada in 1939, and he ordered all the major industries to stop making civilian products and start building ammunition.

Ford and General Motors were building army trucks and tanks. Massey Harris and McCormick Deering were building guns. Acme Screw and Gear Company was making bullets and grenades. Willys Overland was building the famous Jeep, which is still built today.

All the young men had gone to war so there was a manpower shortage in these big factories, which meant that the women were needed to work in them. What a change! Within four months there was no unemployment in Canada.

That meant that there was money to buy things again. Kids were showing up at school with new clothes and some even had real lunch pails. In school in those days the news was all about the war. In the stores the toys were guns and tanks and battleships. We even played war games at school.

There were so many men in the army in such a short time, that supplies were running out. They needed blankets for the beds so our school decided to knit afghans for the army.

Our teacher, Mrs. Laugheed, who taught Dad years before, taught us all how to knit. We knitted little squares and then they were joined together to make a blanket. Our school must have made a dozen of these blankets one winter.

THE RATION RAGE

Still, supplies were short, with so many soldiers to provide for, so we were introduced to rationing. There were coupons for sugar, butter, meat, gasoline, and just about anything else you could think of.

Father had the trucking business so he needed more gasoline than he was allotted. He fared well because he did a lot of work for the farmers and some of them didn't drive a car so they paid Father in gas coupons.

Meat was not a problem because we had a few chickens and a cow in the old barn.

Everybody traded coupons just like money even though it was illegal.

An amusing thing happened to our neighbour, George McMaster, concerning rationing.

The McMasters were a large family who emigrated from Scotland years before. I don't know that George was as tight-fisted as Scottish people were reputed to be or not. It was impossible to prove given the fact that the family, like everyone else in those parts, had nothing in the first place.

George enjoyed a practical joke, and this time his wife was the target. The Wartime Prices and Trade Board was put in place by Prime Minister Mackenzie King to police the use of coupons. Inspectors made regular rounds to make sure that no one was hoarding rationed products. Mrs. McMaster had somehow gotten two one hundred-pound bags of sugar before rationing started. She was paranoid that the inspectors would find it. This situation was a perfect scenario for one of George's practical jokes.

The McMasters had just recently had a telephone installed so George decided to try it out when he was in Dundalk. He phoned home and Liz his wife answered the phone. "Hello" George said, "This is the Wartime Prices and Trade Board calling. Just wanted to be sure you were home. I'll be there in about an hour."

George landed home later with a big grin on his face until he found out the joke was on him. His wife had poured all two hundred pounds of sugar down the hole in the outhouse. "Begorra"

George muttered "I guess that one didn't work out, but at least we 'ave a sweet smelling out'ouse."

THE BEAR

There were quite a few beekeepers on the third and fourth lines of Osprey Township. Our log house was on the third line. The beehives attracted a bear one year. The bear would rip them all apart and cause a lot of damage because the hives were always located out in the back fields away from their house or farm animals.

This situation proved ideal for the bear. No one went near the bees more than once a week. However, when the bear began demolishing the beehives, it was decided to hunt him down. In the late afternoon the hunters would hide near one of the bee colonies and wait. It took about a week until the bear showed up at the Arnott Apiaries. Lance Brownridge and Jim Hawes were there. They waited until he got close to the hives and Lance brought him down with one shot from a 303 rifle.

They took the bear to Albert Heron's barn and people from all over came to see the 300 lb. black bear. It was after dark when Dad took us to see the bear. It was exciting to kids like us.

Another episode involving a bear occurred sometime later that fall. Dad was in the transport business and was away a lot. He often had to stay over in Toronto to bring back a load of farm supplies, but we didn't mind him being away. He was often grumpy around home.

One fall evening we were all in bed except Mother. She was making jam for the winter. She made a lot of applesauce and also canned vegetables to prepare for the winter, which was always long and cold in Osprey Township. About 10 o'clock she heard this clomp, clomp, clomp, out in the yard. She could hear him sniffing at the door and the windows, which were only three feet above the ground level. She had all this sweet jam cooking on the stove and she was frantic. She was all alone and quite a distance from the nearest neighbour. She considered putting us all up in the attic through a small manhole, but she figured our cries would be even more likely to attract the bear.

She was running around trying to figure out what to do next when the noise outside got fainter and finally died away. Apparently the bear decided that with people home he had better come back another time. Immediately after that Dad bought a rifle, but we were never bothered again. The rifle Dad bought would later serve another purpose as a different type of weapon.

On the hillside between our log house and the Gordon farm there was a groundhog that used to come out and sun himself in the summer. Mother decided that she would take a pot shot at the chuck with the rifle. It appeared that she scored a direct hit, so she went over to investigate. As she approached the groundhog, which had been stunned, it got up to run but Mother brought him down with the butt end of the rifle in typical Davy Crockett style.

WE MOVE TO MAXWELL

My Parental Home in Maxwell where they lived for fifty-four years. It burned to the ground in Feb. 2002

In 1941, Dad bought a new Ford truck. It was the beginning of a major spending spree. He paid less than one thousand dollars for the largest truck Ford built in 1941. This was also the last year they would build any vehicles for civilian use until after the war. In 1941 the war was at its worst.

A year later Dad bought a house in Maxwell. Wow! The spending spree continued! He paid five hundred dollars for the largest house in Maxwell on two acres of land. The house had been vacant for a few years but was in reasonably good repair.

It was built about 1860 or '70 by a doctor who used it as a hospital. The house had five bedrooms and two office rooms, a huge parlour and a large dining room. There was also a large kitchen.

There was a good-sized barn on the property as well as an orchard of about ten trees. We didn't think of the trees as much for bearing fruit as we did for climbing. We were like monkeys, more in the trees than on the ground. The lessons about evolution must have slipped our minds.

When we moved to the big house in Maxwell Prin came along too and kept on producing puppies. Some we gave away and others we had to put to sleep. We would go skating on a sheet of ice nearby and Prin would wait at the edge all day if necessary. She loved to come with us to the old swimming hole in the summer, always on my heels as we walked along.

When we went to school Prin would sit at the road and wait for us, or me, to come home. She was a very gentle dog but not a very good watchdog–she was too friendly. Prin was one of many good things that happened to me during my growing up years. I believe a boy should have a dog as a companion while growing up.

"URBAN" LIFE IN MAXWELL

So we now lived in the big house in the village. But now we had to get used to the business of changing schools. Our new school was Maxwell Public School.

The enrolment in the school was thirty-one students, grades one to eight. The problem was that there were twenty-seven boys and four girls. Maxwell Public School had a reputation of having a rowdy bunch of kids. With three more boys from our family, we changed that. We made it worse!

Our first teacher in Maxwell was Mrs. Seeley. This was the second teacher who had taught my Father years before. She was a good teacher and kept control of the school quite well. When we got a strapping from her we didn't go back for a second one. She was a strong woman and our hand would be sore for hours.

At the beginning of the next term they hired a pretty young girl named Helen. Two of the grade eight boys were sixteen years old and the teacher was only seventeen and petite.

In the few months that Helen was there I think we wrote the book on controlling the teacher.

The girls, being in minority, often suffered the brunt of our deeds. I remember that winter we decided that one girl was too stuck up. Actually she was just scared skinny of the rowdy boys, but we decided that she was stuck up so we had to do something about it. We were all outside at recess, and some of the boys grabbed her. We lifted her skirt and stuffed her underpants full of snow. The squeals were really great!

The teacher tried to find out who did it, but she wouldn't say because she was crying or perhaps she used her better judgment when she thought what might have happened if she ratted. Later on we accepted her and didn't bother her any more.

HOCKEY AS IT SHOULD NOT BE PLAYED

We decided to make an ice rink between the school and the old wood shed. Nobody could afford hockey sticks so we improvised. We ripped boards off the wood shed to serve as hockey sticks. So with frozen pieces of cow manure as a puck, we launched into a career of hockey.

The trouble was, by late winter there were not enough boards left on the shed to keep the woodpile dry. The school board, consisting of three or four of the local farmers, decided that tearing apart community property was a criminal offence so they summoned the local Provincial Police Detachment which consisted of one man in a 1941 black Ford with a spotlight on the driver's side. His name was Mr. Black.

Mr. Black came to the school a few days later to inspect the skeleton that was once a woodshed.

He carefully selected the bigger boys and ordered us to come with him to a private place so we could have a "little talk." That's what he called it.

He decided the boys' cloakroom would be a good place. This was a bad choice because we had a layer of ice on the floor where we played games by tripping each other.

The cops in those days wore leather-soled boots, much like they do today. He slipped on the ice in the cloakroom and he looked like Andy Capp when his wife throws him out of the house. He finally gained his composure and we tried not to laugh. He was not used to dealing with public school kids, so we got a rather awkward lecture. He said that with a lot of boys like our school had, things were bound to get out of hand.

He said that when he saw a group of girls together, they were not likely to get into any mischief, but if he saw a group of boys he prepared for the worst.

After this spiel, I guess he decided he better get down to business, so as he pointed his fingers at us he said, "if I have to come here again, it won't be this easy."

He then proceeded to take our names in his little black book and told us this was our first offence and that a second offence would result in "dire consequences."

As he closed his little black book I got a glimpse of the page he had been writing on. There was not one word on that page! He was a great guy, Mr. Black. We saw him in town a few times after that and he would say "hello" and give us a wink.

THE BIG BANG

Meanwhile back at school, we were trying to educate Helen, our teacher, on how to handle a gang of boys in school. Someone came to school one day with a brilliant idea that if we brought rifle bullets to school and set them on the hot stove, they would blow up. The next day someone brought some bullets to school, and just as recess was ending the last guy in put a couple on the old wood stove. Everyone was back at their school work and the older boys were unusually quiet.

Suddenly there was a BANG!!! It sounded just like a rifle except twice as loud, being inside the school. Immediately there was another rifle crack. Helen, the teacher was scared skinny, she wouldn't dare go near the stove.

A short time later she resigned. She had had enough of S.S. No.11 Maxwell. The bullet holes are still in the ceiling.

The new teacher who came in to finish the term was a nice lady, but she was smart, and smart teachers were not much fun for a gang like us as we finished the rather boring term. In the summer holidays they did major repairs to the woodshed and also some things to the schoolhouse.

That summer I was eleven years old and went to work on a farm for fifty cents a day. I was glad when school started again, as I put in some pretty long days on the farm.

Our new teacher looked just like the "school marms" in the comics. She was homely and stoop-shouldered, with a squeaky voice. It took a while for us to decide just how we were going to "educate" this one.

WASN'T THAT A PARTY

Down the road from the school was a creek and one day we went there for a visit. Leaving the schoolyard was a no-no, which just made the whole thing more fun.

We found a full case of beer in the water that had been left there from the Saturday night dance in the village hall, this being a Monday. We carried the case of beer up and hid it in, of all places, the Anglican Church beside the school. The church door was always open so it was an ideal place to hide the beer. At recess we could hardly wait to get over to the church (I believe this was the only time I was ever in a hurry to get to church).

We didn't know anything about how to drink beer. After shaking the bottles around trying to open them we finally opened one and it fizzed all over us. We drank a few bottles and the bell rang, so we headed back to school reeking of beer.

That day the school Inspector came. I am sure he could smell the beer and probably concluded that the teacher was drinking.

A BALL WITH THE BELL

All the one-room schools in those days had a big school bell that the teacher rang at 9:00 a.m., at the end of recess and at 1:00 p.m. to end the lunch hour.

The teacher rang this bell by means of pulling a rope inside the school. It went around a big wheel and the bell was attached to the wheel. When the rope was pulled it turned the wheel and rang the bell. Once again we got together to figure out a way to have some fun, focusing on the bell this time.

One of our gang went up on the roof and tied a rope on the wheel in the opposite direction of the main rope. When the teacher pulled the rope inside the school we would pull against it and the rope wouldn't move. But when she let go of her rope we pulled the rope and rang the bell. She was completely baffled until she found the evidence of our handiwork. After that, our gang planned nothing major for a while. In the summer an occasional baseball might go through a window, but that was all.

Maxwell School House. The woodshed in the storey is on the right. The bell on the top is still there and probably the bullet holes are still in the ceiling.

BASEBALL & CHURCH

Our mother was quite religious, just like our grandmother. I think it stemmed from the fact that my mother's mother died when my mother was very young, so she came to idolize our paternal grandmother who was fanatically religious. She got us all dressed in our monkey suits every Sunday and waltzed us off to church. It was the worst in the summer time because in the field beside our house we had made a baseball field. The neighbour kids would be playing ball and here we were all dressed up and headed for church.

Perhaps we learned something at church that prevented us from committing even worse sins than we did, although the next episode casts serious doubt on our piety.

DUNDALK, HERE WE COME

It was that summer that Mother and Father planned a trip to Niagara Falls. Some friends had invited them to go and spend the weekend there. I am sure Dad hesitated at the word "spend." However, off they went for the week-end and left a neighbour lady to look after us. We got the usual "Don't do this" and "Don't do that" list of rules before they left, but somehow the instructions were soon put on the back burner.

It was Saturday night, the night we always liked to go to Dundalk because there was no school the next day. Well, there was no one to take us but Dad's nearly new truck was available. The baby-sitter went home for a few minutes to do something and that was our chance. We loaded some of the neighbour kids up and headed for Dundalk, ten miles away. There were ten boys in the back and I was the designated driver since I was the oldest. I was eleven years old.

I could barely reach the pedals and look out the windshield at the same time. My brother shifted gears because I had enough to do. We made it to Dundalk safe and sound and after a few minutes of walking around the streets we got in the truck and headed for home. We landed home just fine, but too many eyes had witnessed the episode, so Dad found out soon after they arrived home from Niagara Falls.

We got the usual whipping with the razor strap but this time we decided that we deserved it. Later a neighbour who saw us leave said that we were driving very carefully. I think we went all the way to Dundalk and back in low gear.

In front of Dad's Truck
(circa 1943).
L to R Carl, Stanley,
Clarence, Yours Truly and
Ray. I drove this truck to
Dundalk a few days later.

A GREAT DAY IN HISTORY

We were all working away in our class one day when Reverend Holmes walked in without knocking, and walked right to the front of the school. "Boys and girls" he said, "I have good news for you. The war is over. Germany has surrendered."

We went home early that day and even as kids it was the most exciting thing we had ever seen. People were running out of their houses and hugging each other on the street. It was wild.

That night there was a celebration in the village ball park. They burned Hitler in effigy and cooked hot dogs over a bonfire. It was the first time I had ever seen a hot dog. They were good.

We sang war songs because that is all we knew. There must have been two or three hundred people in the park all singing "There'll always be an England" and "God Save the King" (King George reigned at the time). The village of Maxwell has never had a celebration like that one before or since.

And then the soldiers began returning home. We had a big "Welcome Home" sign when each one of the boys came home.

It was a happy time when a soldier came home, but also a sad time for the parents whose sons would never return, and in our area there were over twenty young men under the age of twenty who gave their lives in the Second World War.

The Canadian Armed Forces were considered to be among the bravest men in the war. The Victoria Cross was the highest award in the war and many Canadians won it.

Canadians were a proud and patriotic people in the post war years. Most of the Canadian troop ships landed in Halifax and the returning soldiers continued their journey by train across the country to their homes.

One story had a soldier disembarking in Halifax and taking a train home to Western Alberta. The train stopped at a train stop in the mountains and, for the soldier it was only three miles over the mountain to his home. It was ninety miles by train around the mountain to his home. He decided to snowshoe the three miles over the mountain. This was easy after some of the marches he had been on in Europe. A week later he went to get his discharge. The sergeant remembered him as the soldier who snowshoed over the mountain.

The Sergeant decided to kid him a little. He said, "I remember you. You couldn't wait to see your wife, so you went over the mountain. Tell me what was the first thing you did when you got home?"

"Sir" replied the soldier "I prefer not to answer that question."

The sergeant laughed and asked, "Okay, what was the second thing you did?"

The soldier stood at attention and looked the sergeant in the eye as he replied, "I took off those damned snowshoes."

Not much exciting happened for a while after the war. I tried my grade eight exams and passed with honours. I really don't know how that happened. It left me in a state of shock, I didn't want any of my friends to know or I would probably be classed as a sissy.

I worked all summer on a farm. I never really had a summer holiday in my young life.

OUR TOYS

As I mentioned earlier there was never much money around while we were growing up, but we learned to live without money. When we wanted something we made it, like my straw filled goalie pads or my first pair of skates. They were made with a pair of Dad's old boots, which were far too big for me, with some old skate blades bolted to the soles.

We made a wagon complete with racks and a tarpaulin just like Dad's truck. The wheels were used from another old wagon. There were parts from a tricycle too. If anyone gave us a toy with wheels on it we would take the wheels off and build our own trucks. I fixed up my own little "workshop" in a back room upstairs in the big house. I spent hours up there making wooden toys. I had very few tools to work with which put me in a category with Dad.

Dad built racks for his trucks and they really looked professional. Almost all the work was done with a dull hand saw and the bolt holes were drilled with an old rusty hand drill. The bolts were tightened with a rusty monkey wrench. My Dad's tool shop was a museum.

I loved to spend time in my workshop, working away alone. I still like to be alone at my hobbies. I built snow plows in the winter, big ones and little ones. I once built one about six feet long and attached a wooden box to it so we could push it. With the plough on the front and a wing mounted on the side, the contraption was heavy, and it took three or four of us to push it. It would clear five feet in one pass.

Every time the weather was stormy we would be out with our snowplows clearing the road to nowhere.

We decided to build an airplane and after about two weeks we had the fuselage looking pretty good...or so we thought. It was time to roll it over and do some work on the underside. It was so heavy; we could barely move it. Finally we got it to roll, and the thing collapsed into a thousand pieces. We decided it was a structural defect. Like the Avro Arrow project, which came years later, our project was laid to rest.

HALLOWEEN

Halloween was one of the big nights of the year in our village and all around the area. This is the night that the kids dress up and go door to door saying "trick or treat" and the friendly people at each house give them a treat.

It was nothing like this while I was growing up. The young population of our town was predominantly boys and it was no trouble to get ten or fifteen of us together. But just as Mr. Black, the OPP officer, said: "when you see a gang of boys together, prepare for the worst."

A couple of local farmers were hostile toward kids playing tricks on them. These farmers became our prime targets. As the saying goes, two heads are better than one. It is difficult to outsmart a gang of kids.

I remember one year we decided to call on Old Bill (that's what we called him). We never wanted to do tricks and then run away. We wanted the farmer to come out and chase us. That was the fun part of the whole thing. By throwing stones at the wood shed we managed to get him out of the house, but he had a shot gun. We were lucky that it was quite dark that night even if the shotgun was just a threat...Hopefully! We were wailing like banshees and hollering like Indians. We said we were going to upset his car and burn his barn and lots of other good things as well. He headed toward the outhouse–everybody had an outhouse in those days– and decided that he would hide in there. If we headed toward the barn he would threaten us with the shotgun.

His plan didn't work out. We waited until he got inside the outhouse. We crept up behind the outhouse and upset it. DOOR DOWN! This pretty well took Old Bill out of the picture so we went somewhere else to stir up some more fun. I still wonder how he got out of that outhouse. He probably crawled through the seat or something. Maybe he even fell in the hole in the ground. A terrible thought, but kind of funny to a gang like us.

Another farm that was a favourite target belonged to a father and son. The son was in his forties and could run pretty fast, so we had to figure out how to keep from getting caught. The first thing was to get them out of the house. They were very afraid of fire so that was the means we used to get them out of the house.

We took a hubcap from a car, put some gasoline in the hubcap, and climbed on top of the haystack by the barn. When we lit the gasoline in the hubcap it looked like the haystack was on fire. This always got them out of the house. While we were doing this, another couple of guys went to a nearby gap in the fence and put the bottom rail in place. We all knew about the bottom rail so we jumped over it, but Freddie, the man who came out of the house running after us, didn't see the bottom rail in the dark. He hit it full force and did about three somersaults. This gave us a head start because we knew this fellow was a pretty good runner.

Another beauty occurred the next year. We found out that a farmer had gone away for the night. This rarely happened around Maxwell because everyone stayed at home on Halloween for the above reasons. Since this farmer was away it gave us plenty of time.

He had a wagon loaded with grain to take to the grist mill the next day. We took the bags of grain off the wagon and took the wagon apart. We climbed on a low hanging roof of the barn and, piece by piece we carried the wagon to the roof peak and reassembled it. We even put part of the load of grain back on the wagon. What a waste of energy! We would never have done anything like that for wages.

And then there was the manure spreader classic. We found a farmer's spreader about half full of manure. We hooked it up to the back of Russell's Chevrolet and headed for Maxwell. When we got to the centre of the big city of Maxwell (population about fifty) we got Amos (you will hear about Amos later) to sit on the manure spreader seat. When we got the car moving he pulled the spreader into gear. Well, ten miles per hour is far too fast for a manure spreader. The manure was flying twenty feet in the air. It was landing on the car towing it and Amos, sitting on the manure spreader seat, was completely covered. He couldn't get off until the car stopped. It seems that the prankster got the worst of this prank.

THE OLD BARN FOUNDATION

Across the road from our house in Maxwell was an old barn foundation. The barn had either burned down or blown down years before. This was a popular gathering place for all the boys in town. Girls were not allowed.

Some of us had seen stunt drivers at the County Fair driving their cars up one ramp and, after flying through the air they landed on another ramp. Sounded like a good idea to try it with bicycles. It turned out that it was not a good idea. We were missing the ramp and bending bike wheels as well as taking the skin off our knees and elbows. Amos got the worst of the deal as usual when his bike went flying in the air and landed on top of him, breaking his glasses. Poor Amos, this was even worse than the manure spreader incident.

The father of one of our gang owned the grocery store in Maxwell, which gave his son Bill access to the cigarettes. Once in a while Bill would come to the barn foundation with a pack of cigarettes, compliments of his father's store. We had erected a "Club House" of sorts with some contraption serving for a stove. I don't know why we bothered with a stove. There was no way to heat that shack. We were heating the whole township.

I believe that the idea of a stove stemmed from the fact that in Bill's father's store there was a pot-bellied stove. At nights a few of the local men would sit around the stove in the store and swap stories and smoke their pipes.

Bill would land at the "Club House" with a pack of cigarettes and I don't know why we smoked them because there was enough smoke in the place without cigarettes.

We got in a little trouble sometimes since we were using a farmer's fence rails for firewood. Many happy times were spent in the "Old Barn Foundation."

MAPLE SYRUP TIME

To anyone who has not experienced the joy of maple syrup time in the spring, I can only say "you don't know what you are missing." Many farmers in the Maxwell area had maple sugar bushes where they made maple syrup in a sugar camp back in the woods. Spring was always one of our favourite times of the year. Winter had loosened its fetters. The water was running in the creeks and ditches. The birds were singing and the whole world was waking up after a long winter sleep. The sunny days would melt some of the snow and there would be frost at night.

It was time to tap the maple trees. One of the great sounds in life is the springtime drip, drip of sap into the buckets.

The farmers would boil the sap in the sugar camps in long flat boiling pans over a wood fire. At night they would fill the pans with sap and bank the fire so that it would burn for part of the night. Just after dark on a moonlit night our group of boys would head out to check the maple syrup camps. The sap would usually be about half boiled and was beginning to have a sweet taste of maple syrup. We would have a drink and we often sat in the shack around the warm fire for a while telling stories. We could have vandalized the shack but we were not vandals. We left nothing but our tracks so the farmers didn't mind our visits.

I don't recall our gang ever committing vandalism (school wood sheds excepted). There was probably a thin line between some of our deeds and vandalism, but we found better ways to have fun than by damaging property.

Making Maple Syrup.

THE OLD SWIMMING HOLE

Across from our house was the Old Barn Foundation, and at the extreme back of the farm a little creek wound its way through the woods and came out in the open fields and ran under the road near our school. This is where we found the case of beer that I mentioned earlier.

The creek was only knee deep in most places so we decided to build a dam and create a swimming hole. It made a great swimming hole but it created a problem by flooding the neighbour's property. The neighbour, being a nice guy didn't cause trouble. He just went and opened our dam. We decided he had no business touching our dam but our parents explained that it was not our property and we should not flood the farmer's fields. We built a smaller dam that didn't overflow the creek banks.

Although I worked most of my summer holidays I managed to spend some time at the Old Swimming Hole. One Sunday my brothers and I were at the swimming hole where we always swam in the buff. Our cousins came to visit us that day, all girls. When they were told we were swimming they wanted to come back and visit us. When they saw us all in our birthday suits they decided to hide our clothes. We were too shy to come out of the water. The girls stayed there for at least an hour before they finally gave us our clothes. There was always a good time at the Old Swimming Hole. Prin would chase squirrels and flush out partridge as she waited for us.

TROUT FISHING ON THE BEAVER RIVER

About one half mile north of our village the Beaver River wound its way into Georgian Bay. It was crystal clear and full of speckled trout when I was a kid. Fishermen came from all over Ontario to fish in the Beaver River.

About that time one specific fisherman caught our eye. His name was Reg Hamilton and he played defence for the Toronto Maple Leafs. He used to visit us when he came to the Beaver to fish. He worked at Ontario Stock Yards in Toronto in the summer because pro hockey wages were not enough to live on in the forties.

Dad, being in the livestock transport business, got to know Mr. Hamilton at the stock yards, so Reg often dropped in when he was in our neck of the woods. This made the Saturday night hockey more exciting than ever.

It was a ritual in those days to listen to Foster Hewitt on Saturday night as he broadcast the Toronto Maple Leaf home games. That is if you were lucky enough to own a radio, which we did. In those days I knew every player on the Leafs: Gus Bodnar, Lorne Carr, Sweeny Schriner, Ted Kennedy, Bob Davidson, Mel Hill, the Metz Brothers, Vic Lynn and Joe Klukay. The defence was Thompson, Mortson, Babe Pratt, Wally Stanowski, Garth Boesch, and our idol Reg Hamilton. In goal was Frank McCool. These guys won the Stanley Cup.

Oh yes, it was every kid's dream to play in the National Hockey League. Hockey was our life and we lived on skates in the winter.

Through the war and in the post war years, Bee Hive Corn Syrup came up with a promotion. If we sent Bee Hive Corn Syrup a label from a tin of corn syrup, they would send us a picture of a hockey player. I had a stack of pictures, mostly of Maple Leaf players. How did I get all the labels? I went door to door and asked for the empty corn syrup tins. In my young mind I was headed for the National Hockey League.

But dreams are dreams, and only one of my friends ever made it to the pros, and he screwed up in his first year. There is mention of him later.

The Beaver River shoreline was densely wooded with evergreens. As a result many fishermen lost their hook and line in the trees when they were casting. This proved to be a good thing for us as kids. We would do whatever it took to get the hooks out of the trees, even if it meant cutting the tree down, a practice not frowned upon in those days. So, with the equipment that we retrieved from the trees, we went fishing and often caught more fish than the experienced anglers.

HIGH SCHOOL

In the fall I started high school and it was a whole new ball game.

We were bussed to High School in Flesherton, a far cry from Maxwell School where there were 30 or so snotty-nosed kids running around.

In Flesherton the kids were dressed nicely and there were about 200 of them. It was intimidating for a kid like me from a one-horse town.

It was not long before I made friends with some guys in my class (Grade nine), and not too long until I made friends with my homeroom teacher, bad friends, that is. Our chemistry didn't mix. She disliked me and I didn't think any better of her. I was definitely not the teacher's pet. Now when I reminisce I bear no grudge—I gave her reason to dislike me.

That summer we had a Field Day, where we competed in races etc. I was not used to this structured kind of competition.

However, in the Field Day I was Junior Champion. I don't know why, other than the fact that through working for the farmers I was in good physical condition. That winter I played hockey in the Intra School League. About that time I became a hockey fanatic.

The depression was over and there was money around but we, as kids, didn't see any. Since we were unaccustomed to having money through the depression years, the lack of it didn't pose a problem. If we wanted something we either made it or did without.

I was now a hockey player but I had no equipment except an old pair of skates that I made up. I had to upgrade my skates if I was to play in the school league, so I found a used pair of skates that I could buy for two dollars. They were excellent skates and I used them for many years. I was once told that they had belonged to a Montreal Canadiens player. Now I had skates and an old hockey stick I found in an arena, but I needed equipment if I was to play hockey.

I found an old piece of Dad's truck tarpaulin and with the help of my Mother's primitive sewing machine I made goalie pads, a chest pad and even mitts, all stuffed with straw. The goalie pads looked surprisingly like the real thing, but they had flaws. Every time a hard shot hit the pads a puff of straw would land on the ice. I soon decided I didn't want to be a goalie, so the pads went to someone else.

I found that I liked to skate with my new skates and I got pretty good on them. When I started to play in the school league I became a defenseman just like "Babe" Pratt, another idol of my younger days. I was never much of a scorer but I could hit and I was a reasonably good skater. When I discovered that I was able to make some pretty good body checks I tended to overplay the part. As a result I watched a lot of the action from the penalty box.

Later I made the All Star Juveniles in Flesherton. We played some exciting games against teams from the surrounding area. I remember one game in Chatsworth when I was on the point. The puck came to me and I let fly. Just as the puck left my stick I fell flat on my butt. I didn't even see the puck go in the net. It was the only goal I scored that winter and I did it sitting on the ice.

It was about grade ten in High School that I discovered girls. I should say that I discovered one girl. She was a cute little thing with flaming red hair and a few freckles. Her name was Iona. Now that I had discovered her the problem arose—how was I going to show her that I liked her?

We both rode on the same school bus so I watched my chance to sit with her. Finally I got the chance. I was never so uncomfortable in my life. I thought all my friends were looking directly at me. I didn't say a single word the whole trip home. Finally my chance came again. In our shop period the teacher didn't want two boys together if possible, so he put a boy and a girl together. Well guess who I got to work with? Iona, of course!

We became friends and I would carry her books from the school to the bus as she walked beside me. It was easy, as I usually had no books of my own to carry. I wasn't much for homework. I paid a girl in grade twelve to do my homework. Her weekly fee was twenty-five cents.

Amazingly I always managed to pass my exams. My friends said I must have caught the teacher in bed with a pig or something. On toward the end of Grade ten I mustered up enough courage to hold Iona's hand. After that we sat together on the bus...it was great!

That year I ended up on the High School Football team. I wanted to impress Iona, but I was a total flop—Markdale High School beat us 32 - 0. I will always remember that terrible score. I guess the more you try to forget something the more you remember it. That was the beginning and also the end of my football career.

The following year I missed the first three weeks of grade eleven. I was working for a construction company and my dad had a truck on the job as well. I was making sixty-five cents per hour and my Dad said that it was such good money that I should stay on the job and forget about school. However, against his wishes, I decided to go back.

After losing the first three weeks of grade eleven it was hard to make up what I had missed. I was even forced, as a last resort, to start doing homework. That winter I joined the School Senior Hockey team in the Interscholastic League. (About today's Junior B level).

Our principal was the coach and he was great. The hockey games were one of the good things to happen to me that year. My defense partner was Ranald McMillan, a super star with an insatiable taste for beer, although he was only sixteen. He would smuggle a few beers to the games. One night in Markdale, he started drinking early. In the second period McMillan skated over to the boards in our end and visited some girls, while the play was going on.

Our coach let out a yell at McMillan to come to the box. He benched him for the rest of the second period, but McMillan loved to play hockey and he convinced the coach to let him play the first shift of the third period. Apparently the coach had given him a wake up call because he scored two goals on that shift. He later scored another goal for a hat trick. His nickname was "Punk." Punk went on to play for the Boston Bruins but the booze got him and his career ended early.

Grade twelve was not very eventful. I had no time for girls since grade ten and Iona. She went to another class and I didn't see her much any more. Then there was Pearl. Pearl lived in Feversham, a village about three miles from the village of Maxwell. I didn't even know her until she was in grade ten and I was in grade eleven. We rode on the same bus but I didn't notice her because she had a brother, Eldon, who watched her like a hawk. He always sat with her on the bus, so the rest of us just let them be.

I later heard about her family. Her father had died a few years before and Eldon had appointed himself to take care of his little sister. He overplayed the part and Pearl never had a chance to mix with other kids. She was a beautiful girl, but then, I was only attracted to beautiful girls.

I would say "Hi Pearl, How are you today?" A few greetings later and I could feel something happening between Pearl and myself. She was making excuses to stand or sit beside me when she got a chance. I was trying to do the same, but "big brother's" presence limited our opportunities to be together.

I told her there was a skating party at the Arena in Feversham and that I would see her there. To my surprise she showed up alone. We skated together most of the night. It was great. Afterwards a gang of us went for a ride in a friend's car. Pearl had to sit on my knee. We started a sing-song in the car, including the big song of the day—"Good Night Irene." Pearl was on my knee singing. Wow! Could she sing, but young people have to have some freedom. We got tired of having a chaperone and things eventually cooled off.

FAREWELL F.H.S.

That spring when the birds were singing they seemed to be singing "It's Time To Go." It didn't help knowing that my chances of passing my graduation were, to say the least, very slim. I packed my books and said good-bye to good old Flesherton High School. It was springtime and I had itchy feet, an affliction that would be with me the rest of my life. It was my version of spring fever.

I went home and went to work at Mel Sled's garage in Maxwell, one of the two garages in our village. Mel hired me for a couple of days while he went somewhere. I was still working there three-and-a-half years later.

The other garage was located across the street and was operated by George Long who was the father of four boys about our age. That made nine boys in two families, which was a major contribution to the overwhelming population of boys in our town.

My brother Carl was a friend of George Long. George's sons were always puttering around with old cars and as a result George's tools often went missing.

Carl bought a snowplow when he was quite young and plowed some of the roads in Grey County in the winter. Based on the snow that fell, and still falls in Grey County each winter, he was kept busy.

Carl had a very good collection of tools that he kept in the snowplow. George would often borrow tools from Carl when his own tools went missing. I remember one time George was standing on the road in front of his garage, looking toward the hill on the west side of Maxwell. Someone asked him if there was something wrong. George lit his pipe and after a pause he said he was waiting for Carl to come over the hill because he needed to borrow a wrench.

George once bought an old truck that someone was ready to take to the dump. He brought it home and with some engine repairs and some welding he fashioned a tow truck. He didn't need the tow truck very often so after it sat a few days it wouldn't start. It was a funny sight, the car towing the tow truck.

We had a lot of fun with George. He was a good man and once we got to know him he was one of the best. His main problem was the fact that he was a poor businessman and that means that he was poor financially as well. He never got the nerve to come over to the garage where I worked to borrow tools although my boss would probably have given him anything he needed.

My boss was one of the finest men that I have ever met. He was a sportsman deluxe. He was on our ball team when we won the championship. You will read about that series later. A short time after I started work at Mel Sled's I bought a car. It had been our family car for a number of years and Dad decided to upgrade to a 1940 Buick. Dad sold the 1930 Chevy to me for more than it was worth but I decided I needed a car and this was my only chance since I had almost no money. I paid him a weekly sum until the car was mine.

That summer I met Grace and we used to go out on a Sunday afternoon for a drive in my 1930 Chevy. Sometimes we would go to a Saturday night dance. We had some good times together but for some unknown reason we stopped seeing each other. I saw Grace a year or so later and I asked her if she remembered why we stopped seeing each other and she didn't know. By this time she had a boy friend and I had a girl friend named Shirley.

Grace was a beautiful girl and she reminded me of Elizabeth Taylor with her dark hair and sultry eyes.

Now I was taking Shirley out in my old Chevy. It was fall and the nights were chilly. My car had a manifold heater that was practically useless. As the weather turned colder, Shirley and I nearly froze in that old car. I installed a hot water heater and with the two heaters there was plenty of heat but the cracks around the doors were almost wide enough to walk through. I was heating all of Grey County, but a little ingenuity fixed that. I got a blanket and hung it up just behind the front seat. Now it was quite comfortable in the front seat.

I cut a hole in the blanket so I could see to back up. The back seat was icy cold, making it a perfect place to keep beer and the hole in the blanket served as a refrigerator door. Shirley didn't drink so there was never any beer in the car when Shirley came along.

One weekend the following summer Shirley and I decided to go to Burk's Falls to visit one of her friends. It rained most of the way home and the roof started to leak. We got soaked but Shirley didn't complain. She never complained about anything, although I often gave her a lot to complain about. In those days the rule was that Shirley had to be home by ten-thirty p.m. Heck! These days the kids don't go out until ten-thirty p.m.

Shirley worked as a telephone operator for the little independent telephone company in our area. To give you an idea of the telephone company, a lady in Feversham converted a bedroom in her house to accommodate the switchboard. The lady and Shirley were the only two operators on duty so they worked eight-hour shifts and the other eight hours there was no operator on duty. It was usually the middle of the night.

The switchboard resembled an organ or a piano. It had dozens of plugs attached to wires on the horizontal panel. The vertical board had dozens of holes. When someone wanted to phone a specific friend he or she had to phone "Central" and give the operator the name or number they wanted to phone. "Central" would then connect to the required line by plugging into the right hole on the vertical panel. The phone on the other end would now be connected but it wouldn't ring. "Central" had to ring the number.

Everyone had a special number. Our number at home was four, ring-one-one. This meant that "Central" would plug into line four and ring one long ring and one short ring, repeating until someone answered. "Central" also had to write down each call so the company knew whom to bill. The telephone man came around occasionally to collect the phone bill.

On the evenings when Shirley was working I would sometimes go over and sit and talk. Excuse me; Shirley did most of the talking. Shirley would have made a good politician. She could talk more and say less than any of them.

The telephone lines were not private like they are today. There were sometimes eight or ten telephones on the same line. This meant that everyone on that particular line could listen to all the conversations on that line. All the gossips had a field day listening to their neighbours' business.

It seems that every cloud has a silver lining so the practical jokers had their fun too. They would talk to a friend and spread rumours like "Mr. Jones' house burned down last night."

That kind of thing would spread like wildfire. Shirley was not exactly innocent of that misdemeanour. She sometimes listened to conversations when she was on the switchboard. I suppose it was one way of dealing with the boredom of being alone so much. Many times there was half an hour between phone calls, so we would sit and gab. I was the listener, and I would drive her home at the end of her shift. The old wooden telephone boxes of that era are now valuable as collectors' items.

In the springtime we always tried to arrange to go smelt fishing in the Batteau Creek or the Beaver River where it flowed into Georgian Bay at Thornbury. The smelt didn't run until at least eleven o'clock at night, so our girl friends had an excuse to stay out later during the week or so that the run lasted. We tried to make the smelt run last on into the summer.

These late nights with the girls were great, but we often went home with no fish. This aroused suspicion and we had to call the smelt run officially over until next year.

BASEBALL

Our village decided to sponsor a ball team in the Central League, which was the senior league in the area. My boss Mel was centre field on the team.

In the playoffs I was designated catcher for game one in Singhampton. In those days and even today I loved living on the edge. I padded the back of my glove and I practiced reaching in front of the bat so the bat would hit the tip of my glove instead of the ball. The umpire caught me and threw me out of the game. I think we lost game one.

That series ended up being the most exciting series I ever played in any sport. It was to me just like the 1972 Hockey Series with Canada and the Soviets.

We were in the seventh game of the best of seven series and the score was tied at 8-8 in the bottom of the 9th. We had one out and Wally Long came to the plate. Nobody expected much because he was just an average hitter. On the first pitch from Howard Hammil, Wally blasted it out of the park.

We won the Cup! Everyone in the stands came running on the field. It was scary. They mobbed Wally and it is a wonder he didn't get hurt under that pile of people. It was almost as big a celebration as the day the War ended. But then this could be dubbed as the end of a war as well.

The following spring we put together a baseball team but it was not nearly like the championship team of the year before. We had some exhibition games before the season started. We were playing a pick up team from Wareham, which was just a community with a church, school, and about four houses.

I was at bat and the pitcher threw me a beauty. I was never much of a hitter but on that pitch I made it to third base—or almost made it. The third baseman jumped in the air to catch the ball and I slid under him to touch the base. He came down on my leg and broke it in two places.

I was gone for the summer. It was probably my best hit ever and this had to happen. My baseball hitting in no way rivaled my hitting in hockey.

THE BIG CITY

I worked at the garage for the rest of the next winter. As spring rolled around I got itchy feet once again and decided to look for greener pastures. My apprentice wages at the garage (fourteen dollars a week) were probably a major factor in my thinking. There was just not enough green for my needs, so I left good old Maxwell.

My Dad found me a job in Toronto at a branch of Goodyear Tire where they repaired tires. I was not exactly comfortable with the job because the big city seemed too busy for me. I lived with my brother Ray in a dingy third floor apartment. I got Ray a job where I worked so we were company for each other. Even though I was not comfortable with the big city, interesting things did happen. The following incident comes to mind.

This elderly man was always walking up and down the street in front of our shop. When he met someone he would say "You vant some?" Coming from the country I didn't know what the "some" meant, so I asked him. He wore a huge army greatcoat even in the summer for reasons that he was about to reveal to me. His arms were both lined with wristwatches and the huge pockets were full of condoms. He was a street peddler. I was then, as now, a small time entrepreneur, always willing to make a few extra bucks.

It didn't take me long to see a miniature gold mine with this old geezer. Make that a rubber mine. In the forties sex was a dirty word and young men were shy to buy condoms at the drug store. I bought some condoms, took them home and sold them all. The following week I bought more and soon I had quite a few regular customers. I was making about half my week's wages every weekend. I had condoms in my car pockets and condoms in my jacket pocket, but it seems all good things must come to an end.

My mother's favourite hobby was minding people's business other than her own. She spied my jacket lying on my car seat with bulging pockets. She couldn't resist investigating the bulge. There were at least two-dozen condoms in that pocket! Immediately my girl friend Shirley was the target. Mother called Shirley on the phone and called her a lot of names, which I have discreetly deleted. Shirley didn't know a thing about the condoms; in fact I doubt that she had ever seen a condom.

I was unaware of the phone call, so when I went to see Shirley I had no idea what she was talking about when she accused me of hanging around with some tramp. This marked the beginning of the end of the condom business.

My mother waged a lifelong war against liquor. Once she was bragging to a neighbour that not one drop of alcoholic beverages had ever entered her house. Little did she know that there was a bottle of whiskey hidden in her house at that very moment.

In fact, Mother was so convinced of the sobriety of her household that once, when Stanley came home inebriated, she decided that he was sick with the flu and fussed over him with aspirin and hot pads.

Dad, being in the transport business, had certain drinking buddies. He would bring home an occasional bottle of booze and hide it in the barn. To the best of my knowledge Mother never found it, but my brothers and I had a few happy moments in the old barn when Dad was away. He probably knew that we were stealing his booze, but he didn't say anything lest we squeal about it to Mother.

A CAREER ON THE ROAD

A short time after the condom business folded, I got spring fever and said good-bye to the Toronto job. I had had enough of city life for the time being. I went home and landed a job with McNamara Construction on a paving job near Stayner. I worked for McNamara Construction for a number of years after that on various jobs in different parts of Canada. Doug was the General Superintendent of the Company. You will see his name mentioned often as I moved from job to job. In the early fifties we worked from dawn until dark and all day Saturday.

A bad point of this arrangement was that Friday, being payday, led to Friday night parties. It still amazes me how we could have licked the world on Friday night but come Saturday morning we couldn't have licked a postage stamp. Mother used to brag, "I know my sons weren't drinking last night because they woke up thirsty this morning."

I remember one Saturday morning when I felt that I was on death's doorstep thanks to the Haig brothers of Scotland. My job that day was on the asphalt mixing plant where the heat was overwhelming, even on a cool day. The heat from the hot asphalt made me sick and I threw up on the load in the truck below. That just added to my misery. I am sure anyone driving along that section of Highway #24 could have smelled the Scotch Whiskey in the new asphalt. I swore that I would never drink again and I kept that vow for almost two weeks.

SIMCOE

The Stayner job came to a close about the middle of summer and the crew all moved to Simcoe to start another paving job. It turned out to be a lot of fun since we had come to know each other quite well by now. We were dubbed "McNamara's Band" among other names.

Four of us boarded at a house with a semi-finished upstairs. The furniture consisted of four cots for beds and not much else. The four of us were young and full of whatever young people are full of. We would wrestle and upset everything. They called us the Boarding House Brawlers.

Simcoe is situated in the tobacco country of Southwestern Ontario. This means that there were a lot of transients in the summer, which led to new businesses, some of them a little illegal. One little town near Simcoe was said to have thirty houses. Fifteen were bawdy-houses and the other fifteen were bootleggers.

A STRANGE TRICK OF FATE

It looked like I might get through this job without getting myself into some kind of dilemma. I probably would have been fine if I had not decided to drop into a local Dairy and Ice Cream Bar one evening. How was I to know that driving into a Dairy Bar would lay the groundwork for a life of adventure far beyond my wildest dreams?

It was a beautiful, warm August night, which prompted me to have some ice cream instead of the usual beer.

The Ice Cream Bar was a neat little place. There were a couple of people just leaving as I entered. This left the rather attractive girl behind the counter and myself alone. I ordered some kind of ice cream. She seemed friendly so we talked a little and one thing led to another. I asked her if she would like a ride home at closing time and she accepted my invitation. By now I had managed to find out that she had a name.

So Nancy and I headed out after her shift in the general direction of her home, although I had no idea where she lived. I had a few beers in the car so I asked her if she would like one. She said "sure" so I pulled off the road into a grove of cedars and we opened a beer. We were sitting there listening to the radio with the windows down on that warm summer evening when a car came by and stopped just past my car.

In a twinkling of an eye there were lights blinding us from every angle. A voice at my door asked what we were doing there. I replied that we had just got there moments before. The lights were turned out and I could see there were three policemen with service revolvers drawn and aimed at our heads.

The cop at my window explained that they were looking for three escaped criminals who had killed a policeman. The policeman was Sgt. Eddie Tong. The escapees were Eddie Boyd, Leonard Jackson and a guy named Steve Suchan.

The cop mentioned that they had better go and let us get back at it, whatever "it" was. He didn't say a word about our opened beer. We headed for Nancy's house in silence. The silence was deafening as we mentally rehashed what had happened.

A few nights later I dropped into the Ice Cream Bar again and took Nancy home that evening as well. We drove straight to her house that night. We did the old smooch thing in the car and she went wild. She told me she was in love with me and that I had to meet her parents. When we got into the house there were Grandfather, Grandmother, Mother and Father, along with some kids–probably Nancy's brothers and sisters. Nancy promptly announced that we were getting married.

I almost fell through the floor, but somehow managed to get out of that place and put some distance between us. I believed that this would be the end of the crazy episode but trouble seems to follow me. A few days later some of McNamara's Band dropped into the Ice Cream Bar. Nancy found out who they were and she asked them if they knew Ivan Young. She told them we were getting married soon.

The gang couldn't wait until the next day to see me. They found me that very night and proceeded to tell me their story, which I assume barely resembled Nancy's story. They said that Nancy was pregnant with my baby. They said she had a very good lawyer and was suing me for child support. By this time I had only known Nancy for a little over a week but I was naive. I was raised in the sticks and I believed these guys. They scared the hell out of me! I have since learned that holding hands doesn't cause pregnancy.

The Simcoe job was nearing completion and there were rumours that McNamara had a huge railway job in Labrador. I decided that Labrador would be far enough away that I would be free of all this stuff. I searched out Doug, our Superintendent and I mentioned that I was interested in going to the big job in Labrador. By now Doug had heard about the Nancy episode. News around construction gangs travels like wildfire. He laughed and asked, "Do you think that job is far enough away to hide the trouble you're in? Perhaps you should change your name. Ha Ha!" It was starting to get me down. Even my boss was on me now. He told me to be in the Toronto office the following Monday. That is how I ended up on the railway job in Labrador.

As I look back on my life to the one week that I knew Nancy, I think of the night I turned into the Ice Cream Bar parking lot. If I had not met Nancy I would, in all probability be a Grey County farmer with a dozen kids and struggling to make a living.

As it turned out my life has been one big exciting adventure, some bad but mostly good, and I can thank a girl I only saw twice in my life.

ENROUTE TO THE NORTH SHORE

I boarded the train in Toronto Union Station and headed for Montreal. Since there was a one-night stopover in Montreal, I asked a taxi driver to take me to a good hotel. He pointed across the street "Voila" he said. "Queen Elizabeth Hotel, the best in Maureeawl!"

With that I decided to check it out. I was just a nineteen-year old hick from the sticks. I had never stayed in a hotel before, not even a fleabag. This place was the ultimate, about twelve on a scale of ten. I asked the guy in the tuxedo at the desk what the rate per night was. What he told me nearly floored me. Eighteen Dollars! Hell I had been paying twelve dollars a week for room and board in Simcoe. I decided that I had gone this far so I may as well book the room.

The room was something out of a fairy tale book. The lobby and the huge chandelier and the furniture were, to me, awesome.

I took an elevator to the floor where my room was. I had never seen an elevator before. My room was huge with lavish drapes and beautiful furniture, with a sitting area and a large bed. They told me later that it was a queen bed. The rest of the room appeared fit for a queen as well. The bathroom had a gold plated towel rack and toilet paper holder. The toilet had a padded seat! A far cry from the outhouse at the old log home. There was even a telephone and radio. Television was still a few years away. This was nineteen fifty-two. If this was the real world, I loved it. I hardly slept that night. I gazed out of the window most of the night. The lights of downtown Montreal were spectacular.

The following day I was back on the train heading for Mont Joli on the South Shore of the St. Lawrence. The group that I was working for consisted of four companies joined together in a joint venture. McNamara was the principal on the huge project. The Company had their own airline called Hollinger Ungava Transport. The airline consisted of half a

Hollinger Ungava Canso "flying boat". It sank in Ashawanipi Lake a short time later.

59

dozen World War II DC-3's, a Canso flying boat, a couple of twin Ansons and a Lancaster bomber.

DC3 Cargo plane, our only contact with the outside world during the construction of the QNS&L Railway.

The DC-3's were used to haul freight and passengers. They were almost always overloaded. The Canso was used to land on lakes where the camp had no landing strip. The Ansons were twelve passenger planes and were used by the executive as they went up and down the line. The "Lanky" was converted to a fuel tanker. There were various accidents but miraculously there were no casualties.

One of the DC-3's flew across the St. Lawrence on one engine. Another DC-3 crash-landed in Knob Lake. One of the Ansons crashed in the north woods. All five passengers walked out alive. The Canso ended up at the bottom of Ashawanapi Lake a year later. There were no casualties.

I was personally involved in another weather-related incident on a flight to Knob Lake. This was the so-called airline that our livelihood was dependent upon, a motley crew indeed. We flew in one of these outdated flying craft across the river to Seven Islands on the North Shore, a distance of about one hundred and fifty miles. When we landed in Seven Islands, (The French name is Sept Iles), they took us to base camp at the foot of the railway. It was to go four hundred miles north to the vast ore fields at Knob Lake, through some of the roughest and most forbidding country in Canada. We called it "the land God gave to Cain."

By the time I arrived, some of the right of way was ready for laying the rails. The new railroad would be called the Quebec North Shore and Labrador Railway or the QNS&L Railway. Sept Iles was isolated from the outside world except by boat or aircraft. This was a rough and desolate part of Canada in the fifties.

At Mile Twelve we constructed a huge bridge over the Moisie River Canyon, and immediately after the bridge there was a rock tunnel about half a mile long. Further up the line there was muskeg, lots of it. There were rock cuts and also valleys to cross.

In Base Camp the bunkhouses had four beds per room, two up and two down. We had our supper in the camp kitchen (not dinner, dinner back then was the noon day meal) before we turned in early.

Tomorrow would be our first day of work where most everyone spoke French. I had no idea what my job would be in the morning. I was introduced to my new boss and my assignment for the day was to walk around the repair shop and pretend to look busy. Ever try doing that? It makes a long, trying day. At least a dozen men were doing the same thing and it made no sense to me. However, being a man of few questions, I kept my eyes and ears open and I eventually found out that there was a reason for this.

Our Company had contracted this job on a cost plus basis, which means that the Iron Ore Company was paying McNamara for every man on the project. McNamara paid us about half of the money they got from I.O.C. Pretty neat arrangement, right? At least it was for McNamara.

I was kept on this "job" for about a week or so and was almost getting to like it when Doug, yes the same Doug that sent me here from the Simcoe job, called me in.

After giving me a few barbs about the Nancy thing he said there was a job up the line where they needed an oiler on one of the power shovels. I flew to Mile 115 and was introduced to Alex McIntyre from Halifax. Alex was an older man but we got along well.

We were on night shift, which was great. We got ten cents per hour more on the night shift and there were no bosses around. That extra ten cents brought me up to ninety cents per hour. The job was great and Alex taught me how to keep the big machine greased and oiled.

I developed a pride in the machine and I wanted to learn all about it. About a month later when the gang had gone to the kitchen at midnight I decided to take the controls and operate the shovel. I had watched Alex very carefully and I thought I was doing a pretty good job. Alex came back from dinner and he must have been impressed because every shift after that he let me run the machine for a few minutes.

Winter was closing in on us and we were living in tents. It sounds rough but we had wood floors and a door, but no window. In the middle was a steel drum made into a stove, which did a

61

good job of heating the place. Seven double deck bunks completed the furniture, seven men up top and seven men below. I, as an oiler, had to take an upper bunk. Only operators were allowed a lower bunk.

Hundreds of Italians were brought in right off the boat to do all the undesirable jobs, like operating the jackhammers, cutting firewood for the camp stoves and cleaning the washrooms and bunkhouses. They slept in separate bunkhouses and ate at tables by themselves. They even rode to the job site in a separate vehicle. Segregation was reaching far beyond the Deep South!

I was quickly learning about the real world.

I believe that the engineers chose the most difficult route possible to build a rail line to the ore fields. I didn't realize that Canada had such a difficult and forbidding land within her boundaries.

On the shovel crew we usually worked in the rock and gravel cuts and we had to move the machines from one job to another. Sometimes we travelled fifty miles at a time at a speed of less than one M.P.H. At night a truck from the nearest camp would pick us up and take us to the camp for the night. Next morning we would have breakfast, pick up a brown bag lunch and take off again for a few more miles. The boss told us to take our time and put in some extra hours. I am surprised someone didn't get fired for going too fast.

Alex and I decided to stay there over the Christmas holiday. We got extra pay for working over Christmas. On Christmas Day we had an excellent dinner. There was turkey, ham, cranberry sauce and Christmas pudding. They had Christmas carols playing on a tape recorder–there was too much interference for a radio. I was a little homesick that day but Shirley's letters helped me pass the day.

A short time later Alex decided to go home for a holiday. I ended up with a cocky young operator and we didn't hit it off from day one. A couple of weeks later I decided to take a holiday before all hell broke loose between the operator and myself. By then he had almost totally demolished the machine.

I was home for about two weeks but things were not like they were when I left. Most of my friends were either married or gone away to work. A few years ago these guys were my old condom customers.

About the only one still at home was Shirley and she was glad to see me, probably because it gave her arm a rest from writing letters. I must say I appreciated her letters when I was on the railroad line. After a couple of weeks I was happy to go back to the job on the North Shore. By this time I pretty well had the feel of living in bunkhouses. It was like coming back home.

Alex never came back from his holiday. Rumour had it that he went on a drinking spree in Halifax and died from alcohol related health problems.

I ended up as an oiler for a big jovial man in his sixties named Henry, who came from some place near Amherst, Nova Scotia. He was a great operator and he taught me a lot about shovels, draglines, backhoes etc. We worked together for about five months on that job. Some things worthy of mention happened in the five months as we worked in different camps.

A sleeping tent in one camp caught fire one night and eleven Italians died in the fire. In the forties and fifties construction employees didn't have good working conditions.

There was no union back then. The small camps on our job had no fire fighting equipment or first aid station. In the line of medical supplies the Commissary would have cough syrup, aspirin and a few bandages. That was about it.

These conditions didn't bother most of the men. After all most of us had survived the Great Depression. This was living in luxury compared to those years.

On one job our shovel was working in a rock cut and on that job there was a little shelter hut where we could eat our midday meal. It had a stove and was quite warm.

One of the men decided to go hunting ptarmigan, a white Arctic partridge. He must have smuggled his rifle in because firearms were prohibited on Indian reserve property. He came back with half a dozen ptarmigan. We cleaned them, and someone got carrots, potatoes, onions and some seasoning from the camp kitchen. We made ptarmigan stew and it was great, the best meal I had in a long time.

Ptarmigan are interesting birds and are very intelligent. They were not afraid of people, possibly because they had never seen people before. One day I tossed a snowball at a ptarmigan sitting on a log and he just jumped to one side. I threw another snowball and he hopped aside again. He was playing a game with me.

While Henry and I were still working together a company plane crashed in the wilderness. We found out that it was some of the top officials on the job, including my old friend Doug and a guy from Thessalon, Ontario, that we called Tubby.

Everyone was anxious and we kept listening for news. Each day hope dimmed a little more. Suddenly after five days in the bush, five men walked into a forest ranger outpost. Tubby had led them out of the bush. He was later awarded a life saving medal from the Governor General.

After that every time I saw Tubby I would ask him about the ordeal in the bush. Tubby would stop work and go through the whole story, which took over half an hour. That meant I didn't have to work while Tubby related the whole story. It was interesting because each time his story was quite different but I would never argue with him. He was a lot bigger than I was.

After all this Henry and I moved our shovel as far north as Mile 224. It was starting to feel like spring. The camp at Mile 224 was set up in early winter and when the spring melt came a lot of the buildings began to sink in the muskeg. Water was seeping in on the bunkhouse floors and it was damp. Worst of all, the airstrip had turned to mud. It had been the main means of communication with the outside world.

The camp was quickly running out of supplies and we had about one hundred men in that camp. We stopped working because of the food shortage. The commissary ran out of supplies, including cigarettes, which was tough on the cigarette smokers.

A RIDE TO REMEMBER

Our only way out was an occasional truck moving up or down the line. The railroad right of way was still passable but it was muddy.

A pole truck carrying a load of telegraph poles came up the line and landed at our camp at about three p.m. one afternoon. By four o'clock he was unloaded and ready to head back down the line.

Henry and another operator jumped in the cab. The other shovel oiler and I didn't get the luxury of the cab. We rode on the cross bunk on the back of the truck. We put on lots of clothes and off we went southbound. We were getting pasted with mud from the wheels and it froze on us as soon as it hit. It was black dark at night when we pulled into the camp at Mile 198. I had ridden a distance of twenty-six miles and it took almost two hours. I must have had two inches of mud on my lap and it was frozen solid. As I tried to get down off the truck, I realized I was encased in a frozen cocoon.

With a few bends and kicks I was able to break the mud loose so I could walk. They rushed us to a warm tent where we got warmed up, and put on a change of clothes offered by some of the men in the camp. After that we went to the kitchen tent for some hot soup and then went to bed.

A plane came in to Mile 198 in a couple of days and Henry and I were among the passengers heading south to Seven Islands. We were sitting at the supper table on the day of our arrival and Henry was explaining how terrible it was up there and how we had to ride out of there bouncing along in a truck. He didn't mention that he was in the warm cab and I was riding on the cross bunk on the back getting loaded up with freezing mud.

It happened that across the table there were some men who were heading up to Knob Lake after a holiday. They told us that they were in charge of a sleigh train taking some brand new shovels up to Knob Lake. That caught Henry's attention right away. Brand new shovels and they would need operators. With two-and-a-half cubic yard buckets, these were big machines. Henry nudged me at the table with his elbow but I barely felt it.

Henry said "Wha'd'ya think?" I looked at Henry and said, "Okay, count me in." The next morning (I couldn't sleep much the night before) we went to McNamara's office and got our release slips. There was no pay as our pay cheque went home to our bank. We couldn't spend money up the line. If we needed something we went to the Commissary (every camp had one), got what we wanted, signed for it and it came off our pay cheque before it was sent home to our bank, a pretty neat arrangement.

KNOB LAKE AND BURNT CREEK

We went down the street about a block and into the offices of the Iron Ore Company. Luckily they were hiring so we signed up and they put us on the first plane heading for Knob Lake. The pilot seemed a little nervous as he walked around in the waiting room, chain-smoking cigarettes. However, we got in the old DC-3 and took off.

Imperial Bank of Canada ~ 1953
Burnt creek Labrador

There were three passengers and we sat on fold up seats along the side. In the middle, a load of freight was strapped to the floor all the way up the centre of the plane. As usual the plane was overloaded.

When we got to about Mile 100 we found out why the pilot was nervous. We ran into some turbulence, and the old plane was rocking and flapping its wings like a bird. It looked like we were in for more excitement than we could handle. The plane gave a lurch and some of the cargo broke loose and was flying all over the place. We were in there with it so we hastily got in with the pilot and shut the door.

It was great to land in Knob Lake and I almost kissed the ground.

The town site at Burnt Creek was a pleasant surprise. Almost all of the buildings were Quonset huts and were quite comfortable compared to the tents on the construction line. In Burnt Creek, later named Schefferville, we even had a bank. I was beginning to live like a civilized person again. The kitchen was a Quonset hut as well, and every Wednesday and Saturday they showed ancient movies, but we didn't care. At least we had some nightlife, which was better than the fabricated tales of sex that we listened to down the line.

In the morning we went to work. One of the big shovels had landed by sleigh train a couple of days earlier. The shovels came in three sections on three huge sleds drawn by bulldozers. The sleigh trains travelled four hundred miles to get to Knob Lake, through storms and bad roads. The machines, when assembled would weigh almost one hundred tons.

An American from Bucyrus Erie factory in Columbus, Ohio, was there to supervise the assembling of the machine. But there was a problem. The crane that Iron Ore Company sent up from Seven Islands was not big enough to lift the massive weight, so we had to wait a few days for a second crane. It took two cranes to lift the upper works and cab onto the track chassis. It ended up taking about two weeks to assemble three of these machines.

The first machine was allotted to Henry and myself. It was a beautiful machine and we kept it maintained and in top shape. Henry was fussy and I was obliged to keep the machine properly maintained.

With all of the travelling that we had been doing recently, Shirley's letters were piling up somewhere. When they finally arrived, I had twelve letters all at once.

Some of her letters were getting a little nasty, wondering if I had another woman up there. Heck, I didn't lay eyes on a woman the whole time I was up there. A woman wouldn't be so crazy as to go to such a God-forsaken place.

So, I had to sit down and write Shirley a letter. I didn't want her to stop writing even though, as I mentioned before, she could talk more and say less than any politician.

About a month into the Knob Lake job the boss came to me and asked if I would like to become an operator on a dragline. I jumped at the chance.

I was sent to Howell River camp, which was about twenty miles south of Burnt Creek and Knob Lake. The camp at Howell River was small. The crew consisted of a bulldozer operator, the camp cook, my oiler and myself.

It was a far cry from Burnt Creek town site with no movies and only three other men, all French-speaking. Norm, my

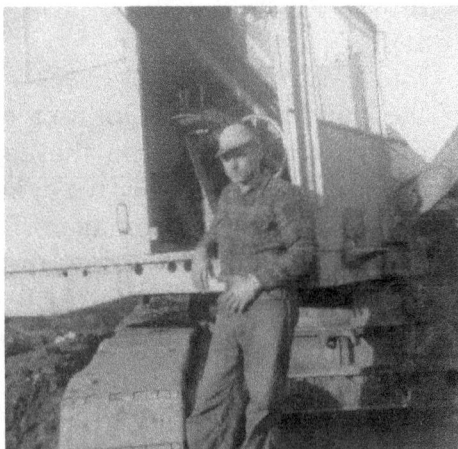

*Yours Truly 1ˢᵗ day as an operator.
Howell River, Labrador*

boss, outlined what I was to do and left for Knob Lake.

I felt lost as a first day operator—and no supervisor except me. The upside of this job was that my wages went from eighty-five cents per hour to one dollar and eighty-five cents. If I were still working down the line I would have qualified for a lower bunk. Up here there were no upper bunks.

I worked at Howell River for about three weeks trimming the slopes in the gravel cuts. I then moved back up to the mine site to live in Burnt Creek town site. A few days after I was called back up to Knob Lake, Henry, who taught me to run power shovels, decided to take a holiday. Guess What! Norm took me out to the new machine that Henry and I had when we first landed in Knob Lake. He asked me if I could handle that big machine. I said "Let me on the seat and you be the judge." He said I did a fine job and this machine was my job now. Henry had let me operate this machine quite a lot and I felt quite comfortable at the controls. I was pretty proud of myself now. I even got a ten-cent raise.

I was thinking life couldn't get any better than this. But it did.

FRIENDS IN HIGH PLACES

The discovery of the vast iron ore fields in Labrador was considered to be a major boost to the Canadian economy. This prompted a visit from the Canadian Prime Minister, The Right Honourable Louis St. Laurent. It was

Stripping overburden at the Ruth Lake 3 ore Fields. I had Prime Minister Louis St. Laurent on this machine with me amid flashing cameras

early spring when the government plane arrived with Louis St. Laurent and his entourage, mainly photographers as well as the Prime Minister's aides.

Neither Knob Lake mine site nor Burnt Creek town site has accommodations for this level of society so they all ate and slept on the aircraft which was, in government tradition, pretty posh!

The President of the Iron Ore Company escorted the group around with the photographers shooting pictures of just about everything.

They stopped at my shovel and the I.O.C. boss came over to my machine with the group. He introduced us all and we shook hands.

As Louis St. Laurent shook my hand he said with a French accent "Pleased to meet you Mister Young." The photographers were setting up tripods as they got the Prime Minister up on the machine standing beside me. They took some pictures as I made one pass with the bucket. Then the Prime Minister sat on the seat and I had to give him a crash course on how to raise the bucket. All the time the cameras were flashing as he slowly raised the big bucket.

70

After they packed up and went on their way, I had to go back to work. This was exciting. The Prime Minister of Canada called me "Mister." It was hard to be humble.

I felt quite comfortable talking with him. If I had not known who he was, I would have taken him for just an ordinary man on the street.

After that day I had good feelings about Louis St. Laurent. I didn't know much about him as Prime Minister but I felt that I knew a little about him as a man, and I was impressed.

By now I had been on the wilderness jobs for over two years give or take a month or so. I was a seasoned Quebec backwoodsman, complete with a beard, a lumberjack shirt and an unedited vocabulary.

LIFE'S A BLAST

I was working in a rock cut with the new 54B shovel near the railhead at Knob Lake on night shift. The blasting crew was drilling up on top of the cut where I was working. One night they had a blast ready to shoot. They said that it was a little way beyond my machine so all I would need to do was turn the rear of the shovel toward the blast. I turned the machine as they instructed and waited.

Finally there was a blast and when it settled down I swung around to go back to work. I started to move the bucket and "Boom" the whole wall of rock in front of me came crashing down. The impact forced the window out of its mooring and it landed on my lap driving me backward off the seat. They found that the dynamite man had used a fuse with a long delay.

He was fired on the spot. I came out of the cab with only a few bumps and bruises and wondering what the hell I was doing up in this God forsaken country in the first place.

The snow started to melt and Lady Spring was smiling down on me again. The black flies were in the millions so I decided to go home for a holiday.

The first Saturday night I was home I decided to take Shirley to a movie. Saturday night was movie night for most of the guys and gals in our area.

The movie theatres in the fifties had a newsreel before the main show started. Shirley and I had just got seated and I looked up at the screen and something caught my eye. It was my shovel in Knob Lake. I was on the seat in plain view, beard and all, and standing beside me with his hand on my shoulder was the Prime Minister of Canada. I don't remember a thing about the show that followed. I was on cloud nine.

The trip home for this holiday had its own memorable incidents.

I flew from Knob Lake straight to Mont Joli on the South Shore in a rickety old DC-3. There was no air service to Montreal until the following day so I decided to look around the town. I dropped into a pub to spend a little time. By then it was about seven p.m., so I decided to take in a nightclub. After all I had been in No Man's Land for almost seven months. Mont Joli in the fifties had many nightclubs. The night entertainment was out of this world. The beautiful French girls with their dark complexions and stylish attire held us all under their spell.

I met a couple of men that I had worked with on the job up at Knob Lake. They were easy to spot because they were about as scruffy looking as I was.

One thing led to another and I ended up missing the plane to Montreal the next day. I got myself gathered up and changed into some clothes that weren't much better than what I had been wearing, but were all I had.

I had looked at a suit earlier and decided that it would look stupid with my beard. I had to decide between the suit and the beard. I chose the beard. I had on a clean lumberjack shirt and a pair of clean but unpressed jeans when I caught the plane for Montreal. I caught the plane this time.

From Montreal to Toronto there was good train service so I landed at Union Station in Toronto at about six p.m. For some ridiculous reason I decided to buy a car to drive home. I took a streetcar to Danforth Avenue, which was known as Motor Car Alley.

I walked into a car lot and a salesman came out and looked at me as if I had just crawled out of the bush, which I had. In my pocket I had a considerable monetary accumulation created by seven months in Knob Lake. I told him I wanted to buy a car. "Oh!" he said, "I have just the car for you." and he took me over to a heap with a half flat tire. How he knew what car was best for me I will never know. Perhaps he had E.S.P. or maybe it was my dishevelled appearance. Whatever it was, I left him standing in the middle of the car lot and went down the street to a Chrysler-Plymouth dealer. I poked around until a salesman came out and I asked him about buying a car. He showed me around the lot pointing out some used junk.

Finally I asked him the price of the new Plymouth in the window. It had all the bells and whistles available in 1953, and it looked like a dream. He said nineteen hundred and ninety five dollars. "Oh!" I said "I'll take it, but only if I can take delivery right now." It was about eight p.m. and we had to get a licence and all that stuff.

He started to write out a sales contract and the first thing he asked me was how much my down payment would be. I said

"Nineteen hundred and ninety five dollars cash." The guy nearly fell off the chair. But I stated again that it was only if I got the car that evening.

I had seen things happen fast, but seldom as fast as what happened that night. He phoned some lady and told her to get down to the licence bureau in ten minutes. He would meet her there on some absolutely urgent business. Usually a salesman will walk from room to room. This bloke was running! Finally he handed me a piece of paper to sign. I looked it over and everything seemed in order so I signed and handed him twenty one hundred dollar bills. (No sales tax in fifty three) It was nearly midnight when I arrived home in Maxwell. I decided to say hello to Mother and Dad even if the hour was late. I walked into their room and turned on the light. I think they thought it was the end of the world. I was still dressed in my lumberjack shirt and had a beard. They didn't even know me until I spoke. I had spent two years, and about seven hundred letters from Shirley, in the Labrador wilderness, so I stayed home for a couple of weeks to get reacquainted with Shirley and also to get used to my new car.

After two weeks I got bored and decided to go see if my old friend Doug had anything in the line of work for me. There were rumblings about the St. Lawrence Seaway starting soon.

THE CORNWALL JOB

Doug told me that they had a paving job in the Cornwall area, which was great for me. I would get to use my new car. For that reason I was happy to have a job in Ontario.

I went to the Cornwall site, and my job was operating a clamshell bucket feeding the asphalt plant. It ended up being another great summer and I stayed out of trouble all year.

Some of us boarded at a renovated cheese house in Osnabruck Centre that summer. We called it the flophouse. It was pretty basic and the food was basic too, but it's an ill wind that blows no good. Right next door the Stewart family operated a general store and they had two beautiful daughters. One thing led to another and I began to see Jean, first on weekends and soon through the week as well. Cupid was shooting arrows but they were not direct hits. Although I really liked Jean, the letters were still coming from Shirley.

I didn't think I could handle two women so I had to make a decision. I ended up writing a "Dear Shirley" letter. At the best it would save her some money on postage stamps. We had been friends for about five years and for most of those years our friendship was maintained through letters, hundreds of letters. Shirley wrote almost every day.

The Cornwall job was completed in the fall and it was time to move on, but my conscience bothered me a little. I felt that I wasn't bad enough to dump two girls in three months. Besides, I really liked Jean and also her family. This prompted me to open a service station in Kemptville, which was a short drive from Jean's house. The service station was a flop but I kept it open until late fall.

Even in a business that is in dire straits and about to close there can be moments of humour.

The local druggist and his wife were nice people, and also good customers at the service station. I recall once when the wife brought her station wagon in. She got out and came in the office. We went on with some friendly talk and finally she said, "Would you have a look at my rear end. My husband thinks it's dry as a bone." I managed to keep my composure. I didn't know whether to put the car or the lady on the hoist.

HURRICANE HAZEL

Hurricane Hazel was a terrible storm! We didn't get it quite as bad in the Cornwall- Ottawa area, but it was pretty scary just the same. When it hit Kemptville about five or six p.m. I brought my car into the service station because trees were falling all over the place. I stayed at the station that night and slept in the car.

This sounds strange that I wouldn't drive a few blocks in a storm. I loved living on the edge, but that night I decided discretion was the better part of valour.

The news said that the Toronto area had been the hardest hit. The phones were out and I had no way of knowing what was going on at home. The next day I went to the boarding house, threw a few belongings in the car and after locking up the station for the last time, I headed for Maxwell. From Kemptville to Maxwell in those days took a little under six hours. There was no McDonald Cartier Freeway back then so I travelled Highway #7.

That trip from the Ottawa Valley to home took me thirteen hours. I had never experienced anything like this before. The devastation was frightening. As I left the Peterborough area the damage kept getting worse, there were trees down, flooded fields and one bridge was almost impassable.

As I was driving through the Holland Marsh a policeman was dragging a baby about a year old out of the mud. Many people died in that terrible storm. Soon after that I came to a concrete bridge that was moved, still intact, about one hundred feet down stream. I turned around and tried another route blocked by trees and mud, another route with a bridge out, and so it went. I drove almost around home before I finally found a road open to Maxwell. There was little or no damage in the Maxwell area except that they had no phone service.

I stayed home about a week. That gave them time to get some of the roads open again. I decided that I had better get back to Kemptville and settle up a few things. I still had some products at the service station to dispose of such as oil, batteries and other shelf items. I also had over five hundred gallons of gasoline in the tanks.

I had heard a story around town about two businessmen who had formed a partnership called Marvan Equipment Sales. They bought used construction equipment and refurbished it for resale. The military base in Fort Chimo, near Goose Bay, Labrador, had closed a few years before and the Government put everything up for sale and I mean everything, even toilet paper–rolls and rolls of it. The two men from Kemptville got the job.

There was no road to Fort Chimo so they rented a ship from Montreal Navigation Company and took a gang of men to Fort Chimo to load the ship. There was mainly construction machinery to be loaded: shovels, cranes, bulldozers, graders, big trucks, little trucks, just about everything, even the kitchen sink.

I sure wanted to go to Chimo, but thanks to my big mouth they kept me in Kemptville. I shot a line about my abilities with machinery etc. so they decided that I was too valuable to go up there and kept me in the home shop.

There is a saying that: "If you can't dazzle them with brilliance, baffle them with bull." When the shipment of machinery docked in Montreal it had to be unloaded by crane so I ended up on the Montreal docks operating a crane. It was bitterly cold that week and it is a wonder that the stevedores who were helping me didn't get pneumonia.

As soon as the equipment arrived in Montreal we started to haul it home with two heavy equipment trucks. These machines had not run for three years so it was our job to rebuild them and paint them up like new. We sold them all over North America to locations as widely dispersed as Texas, New England, and The Maritimes.

A lumber company in Eganville bought a bulldozer from us and I was elected to go to Eganville to give them some operating instructions. I stayed a week back in a logging camp, which brought back memories of the North Shore days. Meanwhile, back at the boarding house I ended up with a roommate, an O.P.P. officer who was transferred from Perth. His anonymous name will be "Bucky" for obvious reasons.

Bucky came from Orillia, which is not far from Maxwell. I learned that he was quite a legend in Orillia. When he first left school he found work in a woolen mill in Barrie. He kept some pretty late nights around Orillia so he was often a little tired in the mornings. He would find a bale of wool in the back room and lie down for a snooze. He said it really pissed him off when they woke him up for coffee break. Finally they fired him and he didn't understand why. He said he didn't do anything. That was an understatement! Nothing worried him.

Anyway, this is who ended up as my roommate. Bucky had a reputation as a good O.P.P. officer. My version of his reputation was slightly different, but he was a great guy and we had some good times together. He was always out of money and not much wonder the way he lived. He knew a couple of bootleggers that he would call on occasionally for a "loan." He told me he liked borrowing a few bucks there because he didn't have to pay it back. He was always borrowing five or ten dollars from me but he always paid me back.

I remember once when he came to the shop where I was working. He was in uniform and the guys all figured I was in trouble. Bucky was an entertainer no matter where he went, and the shop where I worked was no exception. Here he was in the construction shop on his knees, in uniform, begging in front of me. He said: "It hurts my pride but I need ten bucks till payday." Anyway he got a laugh out of the gang.

Later on that fall near Christmas time we were all in bed and about two a.m. his buzzer rang. In those days when a cop was on call they rang his buzzer, he would then phone in for details. He came over to my bed and nudged me awake. "Wanna go for a ride?" he asked. "Some asshole straddled a hydro pole down the road." Two a.m. is not my favourite time to get up, but with Bucky there would be a few laughs. Although I was reluctant, I decided to tag along.

When we got there, Bucky asked the drunk a few questions and then went over to the truck. It was almost totally wrapped around the pole. Bucky started his search of the truck looking for liquor etc. Behind the seat he found a twenty-six-ounce bottle of gin. He carefully tucked it inside his tunic, at the same time hollering over at me. "Well there doesn't appear to be any liquor." He made sure the driver could hear him. By now another cruiser arrived on the scene from Perth. Since the driver was impaired, they had to take him in. There was no holding facility in Kemptville.

The other O.P.P. took off with the drunk in the general direction of Perth. Bucky decided that the truck was okay there until morning, so we took off as well.

About a couple of minutes into our return trip he pulled out the full bottle of gin mumbling, "Cripes I hate this stuff. Why couldn't he have been drinking rye?" He mumbled some more and finally decided that the gin would be okay if we had some tonic water. He turned around and went to one of his friends whom I suspected was a bootlegger. The "friend" got out of bed and gave us half a bottle of tonic water. By this time it was about three a.m.

We popped the lid off the gin and since we had no cups we would take a swig of gin and wash it down with tonic. The first two or three were the worst, after that it got better.

Perth was and still is a nice little town in the Ottawa Valley. Bucky knew a few people there so we would go down occasionally for a weekend spree. I remember one time we had a party at the home of a young couple with a new baby, probably about three weeks old. It came time to go to bed, so Bucky and I just flopped on a pull out couch with our clothes on.

Everything was quiet for a while and suddenly from the bedroom we hear. "Get over to your own side of the bed you damn porcupine." We started laughing, jumped up and the party started all over again.

NEW YEARS IN KEMPTVILLE

That year I came home to Maxwell for Christmas, but since I was scheduled to work between Christmas and New Years I ended up in Kemptville for New Years Eve.

For some reason that I'm unable to remember Jean had other plans, so I picked up a bottle of rum and decided to drop in on a New Years party at a little hall down the street. Guess what! The party was made up mostly of the men that I worked with. I got home two days later. I think we must have called on almost every house in Kemptville the first night, receiving a New Years drink at most of them.

At about four a.m. we were in fine shape so we decided to call on our boss. He was a good sport and got out of bed and poured us all a drink, which we really didn't need. After some more prowling we paid a visit to one of our buddies who had already gone home. We marched in and right upstairs into their bedroom and sat a case of beer and some liquor on the floor. They couldn't get up because they were nude and we had no intention of leaving. We left there about ten a.m., which was probably four hours later.

By this time the booze was wearing off and I was beat from lack of sleep, so as we were walking through the snow in a park I spied a bench. I wiped some of the snow off and sat down. I was asleep in seconds. I woke up sometime later and I was shivering with the cold but I was stone sober. The temperature was about -2 degrees Celsius.

I got up and I could hear revelry on the next street so I stumbled over to see what was going on. It was our gang still "doing houses" up and down the street. We landed at one house about noon and when I smelled the food I realized that I hadn't eaten since last year.

The lady was great. She gave us all something to eat, which was bad because I went outside and brought it all up on the sidewalk. I don't expect in my lifetime to find a more friendly town than Kemptville was back then.

The job rebuilding the heavy equipment was drawing to a close and besides spring was coming. I was starting to get itchy feet so I went over to Osnabruck Centre one night and said goodbye to Jean and headed for home. I had planned to see Jean after I had a holiday but fate changed my plans.

I went home and hung around with the guys for a week or two.

THE QUEEN ELIZABETH WAY JOB

That spring McNamara had a contract on the Q.E.W. from Niagara Falls to Fort Erie. I went and saw my old friend Doug the "super" who sent me to Niagara to operate a shovel.

Some of us found a farmhouse near Stevensville that was taking boarders. The Rasch family had just moved to Ontario from Lloydminister, Saskatchewan, and a few extra dollars in board money was welcome. They had five daughters and two sons. The three oldest girls were Alma, Doreen, and a skinny kid named Ila. Little did I know that, a few years later, one of these girls would change my life forever.

I had a new car and the girls loved to go for a drive, so I told them that if they kept the car washed they could take it for a drive occasionally. It worked both ways. I had a clean car to go home for the weekends and the girls got to ride in it through the week.

I had another great summer. I used to take the girls to the beach for an evening swim and we would all have a good time.

I remember one time when I was on night shift and the rock crusher broke down, so the boss sent us all home. Four of us decided to go to Buffalo in Len's old Studebaker. We got to customs at the Peace Bridge and the old car quit. In those days you needed a border-crossing permit and Len didn't have one, so he folded up a McNamara time slip till it sort of looked like a permit. We all started pushing the car and as we got close to customs Len waved his "permit" and voila! We were in Uncle Sam's country pushing a car through customs using a fake border-crossing permit.

We found someone to give the car a boost. It started and we did a couple of bars before we headed home. At the border the officer asked if we were bringing anything back. Len yelled, "Yeah, but you wouldn't want it. It's not in the bottle any more." The guy waved us through as he muttered "Crazy bums."

CRASHING A "HONEYMOON"

Mike was in his second year of construction that summer. The boss had taught him how to operate a bulldozer, but it seems that his mind was more on a girl back home in the Ottawa Valley than it was on the bulldozer.

Sex was still a very secret and almost shameful thing in the fifties. Mike was really hung up on this girl from his home town so they secretly planned a week in a motel in Niagara Falls. Did he not know that there are no secrets among construction gangs?

We found out the name of the motel and even the room number. About midnight five or six of us "happened" to be driving by and we decided to pay Mike a visit.

We knocked and Mike came and opened the door. We all barged in. Both Mike and his girl were stark naked. She was embarrassed and started to cry. The crying bit was too much so we said good night and left. Mike told us later that she went home the next day. I guess we screwed up a budding romance that time. A short time later I got fired for a "stupid thing" I did on night shift.

A STUPID THING

My job was operating a Northwest shovel feeding a rock crusher on night shift. I preferred night shift because none of the big bosses were around and also there was less traffic on the road we were building.

On that specific job my oiler was able to operate the shovel. I would let him take the controls about ten p.m., then I would whip over to the Montrose Hotel, a distance of about one half mile. I would drop a dollar bill on the table, which in those days bought ten draughts of beer.

On one of these trips to the Montrose, I met a man who had three Redbone hound puppies for sale. I introduced myself and sat down at his table. He was asking fifty dollars each for the pups. We had a few drinks as I kept talking him down in price. After about six beers I had him talked down to two dollars. Two dollars for a pedigreed Redbone hound was a steal, but what was I going to do with a dog?

I took it home to the house where I boarded. Sparky turned out to be a fine dog and they kept him for many years. I sometimes thought we should have named him "Two Bucks."

Meanwhile, back at the Montrose, I would finish my ten draughts of beer and go back to the machine.

I got fired later on that summer because the boss said it was a "stupid thing." I went over to Toronto in the morning to see Doug at head office. He sent me back to the same project but at the Fort Erie end of the job, working for another boss.

The folks at the boarding house didn't even know I had been fired. The Niagara job came to a close in the late fall and I headed home. I decided to stay home that winter and draw unemployment insurance. It turned out to be a bad decision. Collingwood had the nearest beer store to Maxwell, so we spent an occasional evening in Collingwood. It was one of these evenings that Joan entered my life.

BLUE MOUNTAIN SKI RESORT

That winter my pogey cheque was usually spent before I received it, so I found a job at Blue Mountain Ski Resort. Jozo Weider had just started to develop the resort and he always needed extra help on weekends.

My work interfered somewhat with my other weekend activities and as a result I would show up for work sometimes when my name should have been in the obituary of the local paper. I suffered not as much from a hangover as from lack of sleep.

When my shift was finished I would sometimes stop at Joan's house and that would make me late getting home. I remember one early morning I had just turned onto the Maxwell road and I went to sleep at the wheel. My car plowed into the snow bank on the roadside. The car was entirely covered with snow. It would have been impossible to open the doors but I didn't try. I just shut the engine off and slumped on the seat sound asleep.

I woke a few hours later when the car began to shake. My father was driving by and saw the back end of my car protruding out of the snow bank. He had a part load of livestock on the truck so he pulled my car out easily. As he drove away he muttered something about me turning out to be no good unless I changed my ways.

TOO MUCH FUN AND GAMES

I spent most of that winter at home, or at least in the vicinity of home. It would have been better if I had never seen home that winter, although I didn't know this until sometime later in life.

Collingwood, being the nearest town, became a night hangout for the young set. There were always four or five Great Lakes ships in the harbour where they docked for the winter. Each freighter had a custodian who lived on board the ship for the winter. Some of the ships still had some cargo in the hold, hence the custodian.

These young sailors often got bored with the lonely life so occasionally there were parties on board the ship. One winter we got to know a custodian quite well, having visited him on board a number of times. On the ship there were a number of oak kegs of liquor and after a few beers we decided to sample some of the liquor. One of the kegs "sprung a leak" and we found out it was raw rum. It had not been diluted to liquor store standards and it was still the texture of molasses. We diluted some of it with water. That party lasted into the wee hours.

I would be surprised if the custodian didn't get fired when the inspectors came around.

A WINTER OF WOES, DUMB AND DUMBER

That winter there were large sheets of ice in the fields. It was ideal for a skating party. Our gang would pick up our skates and have a midnight skating party in the moonlight. It was a lot of fun. I remember one night when six of us were skating on some ice up in the Blue Mountains. We decided to try another sheet of ice for whatever reason. The grass is always greener on the other side. We all loaded into my new car with our skates on. I wonder if John Labatt had anything to do with this?

The road we were on was a dead end at the top of a hill. I was backing down the hill with my skates on. The windows fogged up from having six people in the car so I opened my door to see where I was going. The door hit a snow bank and because I had my skates on I missed the brake pedal. I bent the door around against the front fender and broke both hinges. We managed to get the door closed and tied it shut with a piece of cord. The door and front fender had to be replaced. Needless to say the skating party came to an abrupt end.

LIFE IS A BASH

One night that winter Joan and I were headed for a dance in Singhampton in my 1955 Plymouth. It was still nearly new despite a few knocks along the way. It was probably the only Saturday night that I didn't have at least one drink.

Just outside of Collingwood a car swerved in front of me and we collided head on. My car, which was lighter than the old LaSalle that hit me, spun around and came to rest in a deep ditch. Joan suffered minor bruises and there were large dents in the dash where my knees had hit. They were pretty badly bruised, but I was able to walk.

The driver of the other car took off running. When the police got there, they easily followed his tracks in the snow. He was charged with impaired driving and I ended up without a car for most of that winter.

THE FROZEN SPUDS

About the end of March that year Dad asked me if I would be available to take a load of potatoes to a food terminal in Toronto. I told him "Sure, Monday morning would be fine."

Saturday night came and one thing led to another and I completely forgot about my agreement for Monday morning. I didn't even know it was Monday morning! I arrived home Tuesday about noon and I might as well have walked into a den of lions.

There was still a lot of snow in Osprey Township so Dad had made arrangements for the farmer to bring his potatoes to the roadside for Monday morning pick up.

Dad was pissed right off. It had gotten cold and the potatoes were all frozen. Dad had to pay for the whole load of potatoes and when Dad had to put out money it was the end of the world. He went into orbit and told me to "Get the hell out."

I packed a few things and climbed into my little Plymouth. By then my wallet was worth more than what was in it. I needed a job so where did I go? I went down the road to Toronto to see what my old friend Dougie had to offer. He still hadn't forgotten the Nancy thing, but after a few jabs he said they needed a couple of operators for a job near Thunder Bay, so I headed out for Terrace Bay.

TERRACE BAY

In the late fifties a highway was proposed between Marathon and Terrace Bay that was to be a section of the new Trans Canada Highway.

A group of Companies joined forces and were awarded the contract. It was a huge job with rock cuts and bridges over the Little Pic River and another bridge over Steel River. Both rivers ran through deep canyons.

About a year into the contract some suspicions of mismanagement surfaced. Government inspectors were sent in, and after an investigation three cabinet ministers were jailed for accepting bribes. Three construction companies were banned for life from bidding on any jobs in Canada. It was known as the "Great Highway Scandal."

All of the construction machines owned by these companies were seized and assembled in a gravel pit near the Little Pic River where some of it is still parked forty-five years later.

When the investigations were completed the project was again put up for bids and McNamara Construction was awarded the new contract. This was spring of 1956.

Terrace Bay is a pulp and paper town between Marathon and what used to be Port Arthur and Fort William, now renamed the Lakehead City of Thunder Bay.

By the summer of 1956 I had spent the better part of five years on the road, literally. My old suitcase, by this time, was beginning to show its age.

My new job was operating a Northwest shovel feeding a rock crusher. A Northwest shovel was known as a "Mae West" in construction circles in those days. It was a tough sturdy machine and it required an operator of the same stature.

The levers had very long strokes prompting one operator to remark that roller skates were needed to operate a Mae West. It was about ten miles from our construction camp at Steel River to the town of Terrace Bay. There was nightlife in Terrace Bay and also in the nearby railroad town of Schreiber.

The weather in the Lakehead area was beautiful in the summer of 1956. We would go hiking on Sundays in the hills along the river by our camp. We once spied a cougar sunning himself on a rock overlooking a cliff. Cougars are shy creatures and he eventually slipped back out of sight into the woods.

Saturday nights were usually spent in Terrace Bay at the Rec Centre.

The town of Terrace Bay was built and owned by Abitibi Paper Company. The workers at the mill were of working age, meaning that they had young families, and it seemed that most of them were girls. A few names I remember are Emma, Freda, Beatrice and Jo Anne.

Before long I was not only going to Terrace Bay on Saturday nights, I was in Terrace Bay on weeknights as well. The reason for this was that my parents had taken a trip and brought my car to Terrace Bay.

They went home by train so now I had my own transportation but, as things turned out, I would have been better off staying back at our camp behaving myself.

LEARNING A LESSON

Our bunkhouse was one long room with about twenty double-deck bunk beds. No one slept on the top bunk. It was where we put our belongings, clothes, books etc. Any beer was stored under the bottom bed. Since I was a little late getting home most nights, it disturbed some of the men who were sleeping. As a result they decided to pass a hint my way that they didn't exactly approve of being awakened in the middle of the night.

I arrived home late one night and there was a "For Sale" sign on my bed. I should have taken the hint but I didn't bother. I just passed it off as a joke. A few nights later I arrived home about one a.m. after a night on the town..

They had tied a rope between my bed and the bed next to mine and loaded the top bunk with empty beer bottles. I was stumbling around in the dark and I hit the rope upsetting the beds. All hell let loose. The beer bottles went flying all over the place. I managed to restore some kind of order and crawled into bed. I was asleep in minutes.

I awoke in the morning to the birds singing and my bed seemed to be somewhat out of level. They had carried me out, bed and all, and sat me on a rock pile outside the door.

I decided it was probably time for me to mend my ways. After that episode if I came in late I just slept in the car.

SOUTHERN COMFORT

Some of us decided later on to leave the camp and move into a boarding house in town. They had double beds and we were told that the rent would be cheaper if we slept two in a bed.

I picked a fellow I knew quite well for my roommate. We ended up at a party one Saturday night in Schreiber and when we got home, we got into bed and my roommate mentioned that he had a bottle of Southern Comfort under the bed. We had a couple of drinks and fell asleep.

We awoke sometime the next morning and the bed was soaked. I looked at him and he looked at me. We were both thinking the same thing and blaming each other. I moved to turn over and I yelled. My back was one huge water blister.

We had laid the Southern Comfort between us and fallen asleep. It had spilled all over the bed. I have never drunk Southern Comfort since. Southern Comfort, in my mind, should be classed as liniment.

That summer my oiler and I picked up a couple of girls in Terrace Bay and we went to the Rossport Fish Derby. Rossport in the fifties had a population of about fifty. When the fish derby was on there were twenty five to thirty thousand people with tents all over the place. One farmer opened up his one hundred-acre farm for parking at one dollar per car. I am sure it was full to overflowing. It was called the world's largest fishing derby.

That fall the Terrace Bay job was drawing to a close so they sent me to Port Arthur to operate a crane. They were building a tunnel under the Kaministiqua River so I looked for a boarding house near the job. The place that I chose was a restaurant called the "House of Denmark." They had rooms to rent and I ate in the restaurant.

The restaurant was a hangout for the young people, most of whom were nice kids and rarely caused trouble. They played the jukebox and some of them danced in an area left open for dancing.

Myrna Loy and Buddy Duval were from Port Arthur. They were singing celebrities in the sixties and cut a number of records.

Myrna was a regular at the House of Denmark when she was not on tour. At the first sign of music on the jukebox she was up singing and dancing and wiggling her cute little behind.

I didn't have to go far for entertainment at the House of Denmark, since I lived right there.

Meanwhile, on the job they gave me an outdated, antiquated crane to operate. Almost every day something went wrong with that machine. The boom fell down on top of a tunnel shaft and narrowly missed some of the workers. As I was crossing a street one day, one of the tracks came off, blocking traffic all morning. I decided to leave that job before I killed someone. I headed back to the boarding house and as I passed the Chrysler dealer one car took my eye—a beautiful 1956 Chrysler loaded with all the toys that were available in 1956.

The Devil started poking me and telling me I needed a new car, which I didn't. My Plymouth was in its infancy. It was about one year old, although it had been through two accidents. I said "What the hell" and succumbed to the taunts of the Devil. I headed for home in a beautiful brand new Chrysler Windsor car.

In Nipigon two girls were hitchhiking so I picked them up for company. They said they were going to Barrie. They had hitchhiked from somewhere in Saskatchewan and by this time they had run out of money. They looked rather unkempt and tired and they were, as I found out later, hungry.

They said that they had not eaten all day so I got them something to eat a short time after we left Nipigon. After they ate they lay down on the seat and slept all the way home. I thought of dumping them out when we got to Long Lac. Then I thought "What the heck, they aren't any bother," so I ended up taking them right to their destination which was Barrie.

Barrie was on my way home so I was not going out of my way. Some company they turned out to be. About the only conversation on the entire trip was their snoring. They slept the entire trip. I didn't even bother to get their names.

CENTRE ISLAND ON A PILEDRIVER

Since I now had a new car on a payment plan, I decided to work that winter. Besides, I was not sure if Dad had mellowed over the frozen potato episode.

McNamara sent me to a pile-driving job on Centre Island in Toronto. What a cold winter it turned out to be! The winds came in off Lake Ontario in bone chilling blasts.

Most of us lived in the old town of Mimico, which is now part of Mississauga. A tugboat named the Ned Hanlon picked us up in the morning and brought us back at night. It had to break through the ice every morning on the first trip to the island.

On Monday mornings the ice was much thicker because there was no traffic over the weekend. The Hanlon would slam into the ice and it would hit the bow and sides with tremendous force.

All of those trips on the Ned Hanlon kindled my love of boats. I sometimes had a feeling of possession. The Ned Hanlon is now a museum piece on the Toronto harbour front, a proud reminder of days gone by.

The crane that I was operating was closed in from the wind but the engine did little to warm the cab. The crane was mounted on a barge, which moved along the edge of the island driving piles to prevent erosion of the shoreline. My crane was on the barge and on the back of the barge there was a shed. Inside the shed was an oil-fired steam boiler that was used to run the pile driver.

It was always warm in the boiler shed and we found lots of excuses to spend a little time away from the frigid temperatures outside. We also found the boiler to be useful in another way as well,

There were hundreds of ducks swimming around near the barge, which gave us a brain wave. We got some fishhooks and baited them with bread. When we threw a line out with the bait on the end it got us a duck every time. We would then clean the ducks and cook them on the steam boiler. We got pretty good at the art of cooking ducks.

This was our version of "Ducks Unlimited."

CROWBAR HOTEL IN PARRY SOUND

That spring McNamara sent me to the Muskokas on a job building a highway from Foote's Bay to Waubaushene. I drove my new Chrysler. One of my passengers had lived for a few years in Parry Sound so we headed there to spend a day before we started work.

As we cruised along the main street of Parry Sound, Don (the person who had lived here before) got me to pull over in front of a tailor shop. Syd and I just went along with him.

As soon as Don got through the door he grabbed the phone out of the tailor's hands and proceeded to beat the tailor with the phone. Blood was flying everywhere. We got out of there fast and headed for the camp at Bala. I couldn't believe Don. He was as cool and calm as could be. I said, "Don, what the hell was that all about?"

Don calmly answered "Well that bastard is living with my ex-wife so every time I'm in town I usually pay him a visit just to be neighbourly."

Great! We had used my car and the tailor got the plate number. A police roadblock down the street brought us to a halt.

After some questioning they loaded all three of us in a cruiser and headed back to Parry Sound. Here I was, my first real look at Parry Sound, and I was seeing it from the slammer. The next morning Syd and I convinced the police that we were completely innocent and they let us go.

Every time I travel through Parry Sound I laugh about my first night in that town. But things were not very funny that night long ago.

A FAILED MARRIAGE

It would have been better if I had never seen home the following winter.

Joan and I were married next spring against everyone's good judgment.

It was a prime example of "love is blind." We were not meant for each other and it was obvious right from the start.

I bought a beautiful trailer home but she preferred to live with her family most of the time for reasons better not mentioned here.

That spring I went to work for a company from Brampton who sent me to a highway job near Sudbury. I had the trailer home specifically for out of town jobs like this but Joan preferred to stay with her family so the new trailer sat idle.

FOREST FIRE IN SUDBURY

In the Sudbury area gases from the nickel mine had killed all the vegetation years before and left miles of barren black rock around Sudbury.

One day a couple of forest rangers came and shut the job down. They picked us all up in trucks and took us to fight a forest fire. A forest fire in Sudbury? There were no trees.

They took us north of Sudbury to a little village that was in the line of fire. There were trees here because we were some distance north of the smelter.

We tried to build firewalls to contain the flames but the embers jumped the firewall. We had to evacuate the village. The fire went over the village and completely wiped it out.

There are few things more terrible than a raging forest fire. It rates right up there with a raging wife. When I came home and told stories about the forest fire in Sudbury everyone laughed: "A forest fire in Sudbury? What did they do, haul trees in to the fire?"

One of my jobs in Sudbury was hauling large boulders out of the bush and leaving them on the roadside. Sounds crazy, right? My company got paid extra for any boulder that measured larger than one cubic yard if it was dug out of the roadbed. Taking them out of the swamp was another story. My boss would keep the highway inspector at the other end of the job while I was performing this dastardly deed.

I had the new Chrysler so I was able to come home every weekend, but I could see things were not as good as they should be at home.

I finished the Sudbury job and came home and went to work for the company in Brampton on a big job building roads in a subdivision. It was close to home so Joan came to live in the trailer.

It was about this time that a son, Larry, was born. I tried to work things out now that we had a family, but when Larry was about a year-and-a-half old we called it quits.

The job in Brampton was seasonal so I was out of work about the time this happened. I don't have much to say about those turbulent two-and-a-half years except it was hell for both of us.

I took my usual pilgrimage to Toronto to see my old friend Doug.

I told him what had happened. His reply was, "Good, I didn't like her anyway." That time he didn't mention anything about the Nancy episode. I was half hoping he would, I needed a lift and a little kidding would have helped.

THE KELSEY POWER DAM

About this time a huge nickel deposit was discovered in Northern Manitoba. McNamara Construction got the contract to build a hydro power plant on the Nelson River to supply power to the new town of Thompson.

It was called the Kelsey Power Development. Doug said they could use me in about a week, so I went home and stumbled around like a zombie while I waited to start work. My life was in a shambles.

I flew to Winnipeg and from there I took the train north past The Pas, Wauboden and numerous other little outposts along the way.

Once I landed on the job site I soon recognized a lot of old faces. I needed that. Big George was the job superintendent and I had been on two or three other jobs with him so it was good to see him.

George and I got kicked out of a hotel in Montreal a few years before so we had something to talk about. He asked me if I wanted to be shovel boss on the job. He said they had eight big shovels in there working on the power dam. "Geez George" I said, "The man that taught me to run a shovel is here. Do you expect me to be his boss?" George laughed and said "Hell, if he says anything we'll throw him in the Nelson River."

Well, Henry was the man in question. He taught me to run a shovel in Knob Lake, Labrador. He said "Go ahead and take the job, I'm happy for you."

So I became shovel boss. They gave me a pickup truck and a warehouse full of shovel parts that I didn't even know the names of.

Some of the other operators I knew were running shovels before I was born and here I was, the Grand Pooh-Bah.

The job itself didn't have a lot of work for me and that was bad. I needed work. I needed to be tired at night till I got my mind straightened out so I made work for myself. I helped the shovel crew change cables, replace clutch bands and grease the machines at night. I guess I didn't look much like a boss but I got cleaned up at night and I slept. Things were starting to look good again.

Down at the edge of our project, near the river, there lived a band of native Indians in homemade tents. They belonged to the Cree Nation, but they were nomads. The reason they camped near the Power Project was obvious. The Department of Indian Affairs stated that we couldn't refuse food to the natives since we were on reservation property.

The cooks gave them food to take home so they lived quite well. A couple of natives even had jobs with our Company. One native employee was Esau Ashkwee. We will talk about him later.

On my job I had a lot of driving around the project as the shovels were spread out all over the place. One day, as I was down near Teepee Town, I saw a couple of older ladies hitch-hiking. There was no place to hitch-hike except the roads inside the Hydro project so I figured they were headed for our kitchen for a handout.

I beckoned to them to get in the back of the pickup truck and we headed toward the kitchen. I had some old bulldozer treads in the back and also a couple of tires. They found a seat on this junk and were happy as could be.

When we got to the kitchen I stopped, expecting them to get out but they had no intentions. I couldn't understand their language but it was obvious they just wanted to go for a ride. It was surely a luxury ride, sitting on an old muddy tire in the back of a truck.

One of our guys left for home but he had a canoe and a 5 HP motor that he wanted to sell so a lad I knew named "Mad Marvin" and I bought the canoe. It was perfect for running up and down the Nelson River. You will hear about Mad Marvin later on in Whitehorse.

Pickerel fishing was excellent and we would go fishing every Sunday, weather permitting.

Sometime in August of that year a forest fire raged through the area. We had to shut down the power project and fight the fire. There are fires and then there are forest fires. Battling a forest fire with a CO_2 tank on my back is definitely not my idea of fun.

This was my second experience with a forest fire as I was involved in the forest fire north of Sudbury a short time earlier.

My throat was sore from the hot burning gases and the fire was eating up oxygen like crazy, making it hard to breath. The noise of a forest fire is terrifying. Forest animals were fleeing ahead of the flames. Predator and prey were fleeing together like friends.

There was another duty to be carried out as well. Teepee Town was right in the path of the fire and had to be relocated on the other side of the river. I loaned my canoe to Esau to help make the move. A couple of days later the danger of the fire had passed, but Esau had not returned the canoe. On Sunday, which was my day off, I decided to get a friend who had a boat and go looking for my canoe.

About a mile up the river just past the new Teepee Town there was someone in mid-stream in a canoe trying to start the motor. That was when I knew it was my canoe. We pulled alongside and I said. "Hi, Esau, what's the matter, out of gas?" Esau hollered back "Yep." and kept right on pulling the rope.

We took Esau home and dragged the canoe back to camp. In the Indian vocabulary I am sure there is no such word as "thanks." They say thank you with their eyes.

A couple of times after that I visited Teepee Town and I was treated like a king. They had just killed a moose a few days before and I was treated to a native feast of moose meat and bannock. They were great people with an interesting culture. I will never forget them, especially Esau.

One day that fall Big George, my boss, had a disagreement with the mechanical supervisor. George hit Louis between the eyes and flattened him right out. Of course that was a definite No-No so they had to send George packing.

This sent shock waves throughout the Company because George was very popular and Louis was just about as unpopular.

A strike ensued and we said we were all quitting unless George was reinstated and Louis got fired. The powers that be called our bluff, much to our embarrassment. About ten of us quit and got on the train with George–the other scabs went back to work.

The train stopped in Wauboden on the way to the Pas. Wauboden was just a whistle stop, but there was a hotel there and a few houses mainly belonging to aboriginals.

We all got off along with George and a party ensued. We almost missed the train and since it only travelled once a week we would have had quite a wait for the next one. When I arrived home I didn't feel like hanging around too long. There were too many bad memories.

I went to Toronto and hired on with C.A. Pitts Construction. I decided not to see Doug at McNamara. I wanted something different for a change. Besides, I didn't need another Nancy spiel.

Pitts had a huge job on the North Shore building a railroad to the Lac Jeannine ore fields not far from the Knob Lake mines.

This job was very much like the railroad job we did with McNamara from Sept Iles to Knob Lake. Pitts gave me a job as shovel mechanic. I was not very long on the job. You will see why later on.

A couple of items worthy of mention happened in the short time that I was there. A bunkhouse burned down but luckily there were no casualties, unlike the fire on the QNS&L project where eleven men died.

A second incident occurred when two thirsty men decided that by straining radiator alcohol through a loaf of bread, it would take out the poison. It didn't work!

A helicopter flew them to the hospital in Sept Iles. One of them suffered brain damage. The second one had no after-effects except for being as stupid as he was in the first place for drinking the stuff.

THE LAST LAUGH

The shovel boss was a man I had worked with on the other railroad job when we were both operators. Most operators are fiercely proud of their operating skills and it is dangerous for them to get into conversation too deeply. A wrong word can cause a heated argument. This is what happened a few years earlier between my new boss and myself.

I foresaw a rather dim future here and I was right. A month later he fired me, which means he got the last laugh.

I got back down to Clarke City, still on the North Shore. Just up the road was Port Cartier, where the head office of Quebec Cartier Mining was located. QCM was the company that was developing the iron ore mine at the railhead.

I hired a taxi to take me from Clarke City to Port Cartier where I went to the office of QCM and hired on as an operator, but they told me there was no bus to Lac Jeannine until late Monday. This was Friday afternoon.

HUNGRY AND BROKE ON THE NORTH SHORE

I had no money except my termination cheque from the Pitts job, and since the bank closed at two p.m. I had no access to my money until some time Monday.

A lady refused to give me a room at the Village Inn because I didn't speak French. I went back to the taxi stand and found the cabby that brought me here. I persuaded him to let me sleep on a bench in the taxi stand at which time I suddenly remembered that I had not eaten for the entire day. Here I was, hungry and broke in this inhospitable place.

Sometime late Saturday afternoon the taxi driver broke down and shared a cheese sandwich with me. His English vocabulary was limited—about the same as my French. We managed to communicate for those two days that seemed to me like an eternity. He was the only friend I had.

Monday finally arrived. It seemed like I had been in the taxi stand for a month.

I got the cabby to take me to the bank to cash my cheque. I then got him to take me to the mess hall at QCM. I paid him for the fare and gave him a ten-dollar tip for being such a nice guy. He nearly fell over, ten dollars was probably half of his weekly pay up there.

I was starving when I got to the mess hall. It was a buffet and I filled my plate to overflowing. My new employer issued me a bunk, but the bus was leaving for the mine site in the afternoon and I wasn't about to miss it.

That afternoon I boarded the bus to Lac Jeannine. New job—new country—life was pretty good. The Lac Jeannine job turned out to be another great experience. Our gang on the night shift maintenance crew was a really super bunch of guys.

One of my first jobs was helping to assemble one of the giant ore shovels. Somewhere I have a picture of a pickup truck in the bucket of that machine.

After the shovels were assembled, our crew was assigned to the night shift. The crew consisted of our boss, Don, a big lanky Scotsman from Ontario. He had worked on the Elliot Lake uranium job before this and it was the exclusive topic of his conversation. Hugh was from Antigonish, Nova Scotia. He was a super mechanic. George was an Anglophone from the town of Asbestos, Quebec. Marcel was a French kid who spoke very little English. I completed the crew and at this particular time seemed to have no fixed address.

Being on the maintenance crew had no happy medium. When one machine broke down Murphy's Law dictated that at least three others would develop a problem at the same time.

There were also many nights when not one call came in. On those nights we just sat in the little shed that was our headquarters and played cards. The shed was heated by a small oil stove, which kept it warm. Sometimes we would get tired of cards and have a nap.

Don stayed in his truck most of the time to be close to the CB in case a call came in.

FUN AND GAMES

We had a lot of good times that winter, telling stories, playing cards, and playing tricks on each other.

I recall one night when I stepped out of the "office" to make an "icicle." There was the boss, Don, fast asleep in his jeep. I rushed back inside and told the crew and in about ten seconds flat we sprang into action.

We found a heavy steel cable and attached it to the rear axle of Don's Jeep. After leaving about forty feet of slack we attached the other end of the cable to a fifty-ton shovel boom directly behind his Jeep.

We then got in our Jeep pickup, and as we got beside Don's truck we blew the horn for Don to follow us. He took off after us for about forty feet and it is a wonder he didn't go through the windshield. It was also a wonder he didn't tear the rear end out from under the pickup. I guess it speaks for the quality of the old Jeep pickups.

We stopped on a hill and watched him slowly get out of his truck and take a wrench out of his tool box and unclamp the cable, after which he carefully rolled the cable up and got back in his truck.

He then took a drive around the mine site. This was open pit mining so there were roads right into the mine where the big machines were working.

We were more than a little apprehensive about meeting Don in the morning. We went in to make out our time slips and the first person we met was Don. "Hi guys" he smiled, "see you next shift." We couldn't believe our good luck, not one word about the cable.

A couple of nights later we found out why. We were sitting in the shop telling stories and playing cards when Don walked in. "Hi guys" he said. "Lets take a drive around the mine site just to let them know that we're still around."

Hugh and I were mechanics and the other two on the crew were helpers, so we left the helpers at the shop. Were they ever lucky!

We went out and hopped into Don's truck and started off, but both windows were down. It was bitterly cold and we had left our heavy parkas in the shop. I tried to roll the window up but the window winder was gone. That was when things started to add up. We were sitting there almost too stiff to shiver. Don looked over at us and said: "Whatsamatter guys, can't handle the cold? Doesn't bother me, I'm the outdoor type. Outdoor type! Yeah! Right! He had more clothes on than I owned.

When we got back to the shop Hugh and I couldn't stop shivering for the rest of the night. I shiver yet when I think of that night.

I was there about three months when they discovered that I could operate a shovel so they stuck me on one of those eight cubic yard monsters. That shovel was a joy to run. Air conditioned and soundproof, it had all the bells and whistles.

There was one thing I missed. I missed the nonsense of the old gang as I sat way up there all alone for ten hours.

I stayed on that job for over six months before I decided to take a holiday. By now I had all my debts paid off from the marriage breakup and I was feeling pretty good.

I got on a bus one day and headed for Seven Islands, the town that I knew from the Knob Lake job. It was just down the road from Port Cartier still on the North Shore. I met some old friends and one thing led to another. I ended up staying a couple of days.

Seven Islands was a great little town in the sixties. It had plenty of nightclubs and restaurants. It was a good town for transients to hang out in.

Being a transient myself, I felt right at home in Sept Iles. French entertainment is the very best. The French singers were beautiful, both in body and voice. The male singers were good, but I had not laid eyes on a woman in over six months so the ladies took centre stage.

The clubs served "good to the last drop drinks." We transients dropped a lot of money on the North Shore in the fifties and sixties.

I went home for a couple of weeks, but most of my friends were gone. There was just nothing to keep young people at home in the village of Maxwell. After two weeks I was bored, so once again I went to see Doug at McNamara. He signed me up for a job in Fort Churchill and I was off again, this time to Northern Manitoba.

STRATEGIC AIR COMMAND, FORT CHURCHILL

McNamara had a contract in Fort Churchill to extend the airstrip to accommodate the giant B.52 bombers of the US Air Force. SAC manned Fort Churchill during the Cold War years.

We had a fleet of motor scrapers in Fort Churchill hauling sand from a beach on Hudson Bay. The sand was frozen below the surface, so we would scrape a layer off the top. The sun would melt another layer and we would start over again a few days later. The sandpit on the beach had to be over a mile square for the sun to melt enough area to keep the big machines busy.

My job was night shift mechanic on the big earthmovers. I recall one night when "Cowboy Jim" (we often had crazy names for each other) was rolling along with a full load on one of the earthmovers. He hit a pothole in the roadway and broke the cable holding the scraper blade up. The blade hit the road and everything stopped dead.

Cowboy Jim was thrown against the windshield. He came out of the cab with a broken nose and spitting blood, having put his teeth through his lip. We took him to the Air Force first aid post and a nurse patched him up. Jim came back and finished the shift!

Sympathy on construction jobs in those days was nonexistent. We called him Fat Lips and said he looked better hiding behind the bandage on his nose. We told him if he was looking for sympathy he would probably find it in the dictionary. Jim was one of the boys and we knew we could kid around with him even if he was much bigger than most of us.

Down the road a short distance from Fort Churchill was the town of Churchill. There were three hotels in Churchill, which made it a favourite hangout for our gang and also the Air Force guys.

Churchill was the grain terminal for most of the Western wheat. Hundreds of grain cars were lined up in the railroad yard, waiting to unload at the elevators.

Ships from all over the world came here to load up with western wheat. As a result, sailors from all over the world spent a little shore time in one of three hotel bars in Churchill.

I was with a couple of buddies one day and we dropped in for a thirst quencher. Nearby there were a couple of tables occupied by Portuguese sailors. We didn't understand the language but there appeared to be an argument. Suddenly two of them stood up and quick as a flash of lightning they bent down to their high boots and came up with knives. We suddenly decided that we had business elsewhere, so we left leaving half a beer on the table.

In Manitoba it was legal to buy a case of beer after twelve at night.

One night we were in town and when the bar closed we bought a couple of cases of beer to take home. We set the beer down and waited for a taxi. When we picked the beer cases up they were almost empty. The natives had slipped the beer out of the cases and were long gone. After that when we got a case of beer we sat on it until the taxi arrived.

Churchill was very barren. There were no trees and very little vegetation of any kind. Governed by the wind, the ice would come and go along the shore.

One time there would be ocean as far as the eye could see. The next day there would be a solid mass of ice as far as you could see. The polar bears rode the ice floes. There were a lot of bears in the Churchill area, and "beware of the bears" signs were posted everywhere.

The Department of Indian Affairs built a town site for the natives. About twelve houses were given to the Eskimos and another dozen were given to the Indian people. It was not difficult to tell the Indian houses from the Eskimo houses.

The Eskimo houses were kept neat and nicely painted. They even tried to grow shrubs in the yard. The Indians would take the boards off the outside of their houses and burn them in the stoves inside. When the weather got cold they would cover the walls with sealskin, which they sold to the fur traders in the spring.

Just outside the town was the Adanac Whaling Company's factory. In the spring thousands of White Beluga whales converged in the mouth of the Churchill River. The natives speared them and sold them to the whaling factory.

The whales were dragged up on shore and left there for the factory workers to process the oil. Some of the whales lay on the shore for a month before they were taken into the factory. You can imagine the disgusting smell, but apparently it didn't affect the whale oil that was extracted.

Imagine Aboriginal men and women working under these conditions day after day for very little wages. I could hardly stand to walk past the place because of the terrible stench.

BACK IN HOGTOWN

I came home and hung around for about two weeks before I landed a job in Toronto with Scott Jackson Construction. They were building a trunk sewer system in the Don River Valley in Leaside, a suburb of Toronto.

It was a good job except for one thing. It was in the city, and I had a thing about city life.

We had a bulldozer operator who was in his sixties and we called him "Hambone" or sometimes "Hammer" for short. Now Hambone was a legend among construction companies in Toronto and for a good reason.

He was a great old man but he was his own worst enemy. Hambone would drink anytime of the day or night. The Italians on the job brought homemade wine to work to drink with their lunch. Hambone would find it and be drunk by noon. After he slept for an hour he was ready to go right back to work as if nothing had happened.

Hambone rode to work with me, so occasionally we dropped into the Cloverleaf Hotel for a drink on the way home. One time Hammer apparently was extra thirsty. By the time I was ready to go he was bombed. I could see a problem getting him to my car so I went over and tapped him on the shoulder.

In his drunken state he considered this a challenge to a fight. He tried to get up but he just couldn't control his arms and legs. He took off backwards knocking over tables and chairs. With the help of a waiter, I got him gathered up and loaded into my car.

Hammer had lost his driving licence many years before and just never bothered to try and get it back, which is why he rode with me. I drove up to his house and his ninety-year-old mother came out with a broom and took after me for getting her son drunk. Boy, could she cuss!

It was a little later on that a buddy and I decided to go to Buffalo for the weekend for a change of scenery.

On our way to Buffalo I decided to call on the Rasch family in Stevensville and say "Hello." This is the family where I boarded when we did the highway job on the Queen Elizabeth Way.

Some of the family was still living at home. They told me that Ila was in the RCAF in Trenton. Ila was the skinny sixteen-year-old when I boarded at the Rasch house.

A few weeks later my buddy and I were headed east on Highway #2 on our way to Montreal for the weekend. I decided to call on Ila in Trenton.

When I saw her she took my breath away. From age sixteen to age twenty-one there had been a breathtaking change from a skinny kid to a beautiful woman. Wow! I started to see her on weekends. Trenton was not far from Toronto where I worked so I was able to spend a few weekends in Trenton.

Ila (her nickname was and still is "Sue") had a touch of fun loving Danish mischief that came from her ancestry.

For a number of reasons I wondered if Sue was right for me. I was not yet divorced and Sue was young and had her life ahead of her. I chose not to get involved and spoil her young life.

Somewhere in my travels I met a German girl named Hannah who lived in East Toronto. Like me she had been married before. She had two young children.

We started to see each other and ended up renting a house in Scarborough. I was hoping to have some kind of life with her and the kids and let the girl in Trenton find a decent guy.

The Scarborough romance didn't last long. Hannah was a gold digger and liked the society life. I simply didn't fit into that kind of a life style. I was not long in finding out that this arrangement wasn't going to work, so I packed my bags and was on the road again.

I bade my employer, Scott Jackson, good-bye and was ready to embark on another adventure somewhere with my old friend and travel companion, my suitcase.

I received a letter from "Mad Marvin" in the Yukon bearing news of what appeared to be an interesting opportunity. This was the same Mad Marvin that I canoed with on the Nelson River in Northern Manitoba. He told me that a company in Whitehorse was looking for a shovel operator. I decided to check it out. Surely my old suitcase would last through one more adventure.

THE SPELL OF THE YUKON

I left Toronto just before Christmas of 1962. Among other things, I had had enough of city life. Mad Marvin said a Company from Edmonton had a job near Whitehorse so I bought an airline ticket and was off to the Yukon.

I became ill on the aircraft and when we reached Whitehorse they plunked me in the hospital. I got out of the hospital a few days later, but since the job was already filled I was unemployed. I looked Mad Marvin up and he said I could stay at his place with him and his brand new bride. When I saw the place they were living in I got the surprise of my life.

The place was a half-finished row house and when I say half-finished I mean less than half-finished. On the inside were stud walls and the place had no doors or windows. A piece of white plastic covered the hole where a window should have been and about three blankets hung down in the doorway. It had a wood stove, which kept it reasonably livable. His wife was living in this place with him. Unbelievable!

I stayed with them in that place for about a week before I found a cabin for rent in the north end of Whitehorse. It had a kitchen, a sitting room and one bedroom. It also had all the basic furnishings and was heated by an oil-stove. I moved Mad Marvin and his new wife in with me, but by this time his wife was fed up with living like this so she went home to Winnipeg and left Marvin in Whitehorse. It was no life for a young woman.

Although our cabin was rather basic it was certainly better than the place we came from, and I lived there during my entire stay in Whitehorse.

DAILY TRIPS TO THE RIVER

In the area of Whitehorse where we lived the houses had no running water. The Yukon River was nearby, so it was the source of our water supply. The problem was that in the winter the river froze over. This meant that someone had to chop a hole in the ice to get water.

I was usually up early so I would go to the river and chop a hole in the ice and get a pail of water. It was not long until I realized how dumb I was. The neighbours all waited until I broke the hole open and then they would all head for the water hole, pail in hand.

I decided to play the waiting game too. I would watch out the window for someone to break down and be first to the river. I met a lot of friends during those trips to the water hole.

Mad Marvin drove a taxi on night shift and I drove taxi part time, usually on days. Before I was allowed to drive a taxi there were a few stipulations involved.

One was that I was required to have a case of whiskey. Six bottles were to be regular and six bottles were to be diluted with water to half strength, making it twelve bottles instead of six. It was to be sold to the aboriginals for the same price as the good whiskey. But I had a problem; I didn't have sixty dollars, the price of a case of liquor.

Mad Marvin told me to go down to the liquor store and negotiate. I was less than five minutes in the liquor store when I came out with a case of whiskey that I was supposed to pay for on pogey day.

Now I was a "registered" taxi driver. This was the way it was in Whitehorse. Everybody was so laid back and friendly.

If you met anyone on the street, friend or stranger, you greeted him or her with a "hello," or sometimes a handshake. It was the same in bars and restaurants.

I remember one little restaurant where I went occasionally. They had a slogan on the wall which said "You Are A Stranger Here But Once." That little slogan said it all.

RECOLLECTIONS OF A HACK DRIVER

An American hunting party once hired my taxi for a day of hunting, but it ended up to be more drinking than hunting. I took them up toward Carmacks to an area where there was supposed to be wildlife. We didn't see any game, for which I was glad. These fellows were in no state to handle a rifle.

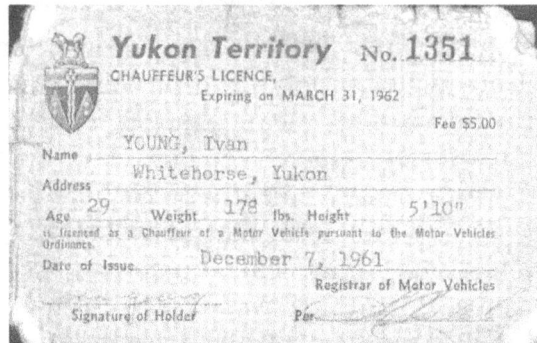

Yukon Territory No. 1351
CHAUFFEUR'S LICENCE,
Expiring on MARCH 31, 1962
Fee $5.00
Name   YOUNG, Ivan
Address   Whitehorse, Yukon
Age 29   Weight 178 lbs. Height   5'10"
is licensed as a Chauffeur of a Motor Vehicle pursuant to the Motor Vehicles Ordinance.
Date of Issue   December 7, 1961
Registrar of Motor Vehicles
Signature of Holder   Per

When the day was over they gave me one hundred dollars American and told me to keep the whiskey. One of them had no money to pay his share of the taxi fare so he gave me his rifle. What a rifle—a 270-BSA with a Monte Carlo stock and fitted with a scope! That rifle was worth a fortune.

I graciously told him that he could redeem the rifle if he was later able to come up with the money. I never saw them again so I planned to keep the rifle, but somewhere in my travels I ran out of money and had to reluctantly leave the rifle in the same way that I inherited it.

This was the way it was in the taxi business in Whitehorse. We often traded goods instead of money. When we took an Indian home after the bars closed he would usually buy a bottle of our watered down whiskey and if he had no money, which was often, we would negotiate a deal. Often we accepted a guitar, violin, axe, rifle, you name it, in payment. They were told that they could redeem these items later but few of them ever came back. As a result our cabin walls were lined with all this loot. It was beginning to weigh heavy on our pocket book. We tried to sell it but few people had money to buy it.

I often ended up spending evenings alone in the cabin due to the lack of money. I was at home one evening, short of cash, and I got bored listening to the staccato reception on the radio. (Reception was not very good in Whitehorse). I decided to take a stroll down to the taxi stand and try to get into a game of cards.

As I was passing one place, a man came out of the house to go to the bathroom. He spied me walking and came running over and grabbed my hand and dragged me into the house to a party. I didn't know the man nor did I know anyone else in the house. What a party! I left that house two days later. I never did get to the taxi stand for a card game. I don't believe anyone went looking for me during the two days that I went missing, a rather scary thought.

This was just before Christmas and I decided to cook up a decent Christmas dinner for Marv and myself even if he didn't bother to look for me when I was AWOL. I put on my army greatcoat and went down to the Northern Commercial store to do some shopping. I picked up a couple of big steaks and put them in the pockets of my greatcoat. I also picked up some potatoes, onions and carrots, which I paid for. The steaks, I decided were a Christmas gift from Northern Commercial. Lack of money and hunger can sometimes make a person change one's way of thinking.

A YUKON CHRISTMAS

On Christmas day Mad Marvin went down to the taxi stand for a while. I told him I was cooking Christmas dinner if he happened to be around about noon.

Our kitchen stove was an electric hot plate and around noon I started to cook dinner. I had everything going great in anticipation of a good Christmas dinner when the power went off. I'm standing there cussing about ruining the Christmas dinner saying that this was my penalty for stealing steaks when a knock came to the door.

I opened the door and there stood a tall Mountie. My first thought was "Oh shit, they caught me stealing steaks." The Mountie explained to me that the whole main street of Whitehorse was on fire and he was recruiting people to fight the fire. The hydrants were all frozen.

I got my coat, hopped in the cruiser and he took me to the fire scene. They put me on the bucket brigade where they were handing buckets of snow from hand to hand right up to the top of a flat-topped building across the street from the fire. The snow melted and kept the front of the stores wet so they wouldn't catch fire in the tremendous heat. The man who emptied the bucket would then go to the back of the line. It was a terrible fire.

I began to believe that I was prone to fires, two forest fires and now this. As soon as I got to the roof I dumped my bucket and hurried back out of the heat.

I spied Mad Marvin down there with the taxi so I ran over and hid in the back seat. I'd had enough of the fire. Marvin took me to a settlement called Whiskey Flats, to another taxi driver's place.

I stayed there until the fire was over. The next day we went down to see what was left of Main Street. It had burned out seven businesses in Downtown Whitehorse. "Merry" Christmas 1962.

THE LUMBERJACKS

One cold day just after New Years I took my pogey cheque and, since I had nothing else to do, I headed downtown. My first stop was at the liquor store where I paid my liquor bill. The last thing I wanted was to ruin my credit at the liquor store.

I then decided to drop in to the "98" hotel and catch up on the local gossip, while sampling a Molson Golden. I sat down and ordered a drink. At the tables nearby there was a gang of lumberjacks who had just blown into town out of the Yukon backwoods. These guys were tough and hardy, a condition necessary to survive in the Yukon winters. Some of them wore lumberjack plaid shirts and they were bare-chested right to the belt line. This was January and we were in the Yukon.

They were getting rather loud, an indication that they had been there for a while already. Eventually one of these guys got up and flexed his muscles and announced. "I am the toughest man in the Yukon." Everybody laughed and when the laughter subsided a huge man at the next table got up. He hit the braggart so hard that the guy went backwards and upset some empty tables before he fell down. The big man yelled, "There, that makes you the second toughest man in the Yukon."

Having said that he walked over and helped the guy up, after which they sat down together at a table and ordered a drink.

This was how these lumberjacks played. The bartender knew better than to try to throw them out so he brought the drinks.

About a week or so later I learned about a construction company that was interviewing people to work on a bridge job near Dawson City.

The interviews were in Whitehorse. I went down and gave Mr. Rice my usual line of B.S. and he hired me on the spot. It would be a week before they needed me.

While in Whitehorse I made friends with a girl named Helen, who moved there from Grand Prairie after her marriage failed. She was a nice person and I liked talking to her, but I still couldn't forget the girl in Trenton so Helen remained just a friend.

I told her that I was going up to Dawson City to work. She made a big fuss and said she would miss me. Heck I hardly even knew her.

I was still a taxi driver because it would be a few days before I was to go north to the bridge job. About a couple of nights later I was in the taxi stand. The phone rang and it was Helen, and she was bombed. She wanted me to pick her up at Tourist Service Motel and take her home.

I drove over and didn't bother to knock. I just walked in. The sight that I saw was not for the faint of heart. Lying on the bed was a big girl they called Babs. I had only seen her once before. She was lying passed out beside some guy and they were both stark naked.

There was a man slumped down in a corner, passed out with his winter clothes and boots still on. There was quite a contrast from the bed to that corner.

Helen was crawling around under the bed looking for her purse, which was hanging on her shoulder.

On the night table stood a one-gallon can of Alaska Moonshine. Any further explanation of the above spectacle is deemed unnecessary. I managed to get Helen out of there and into the taxi. She was all over me so much that I could hardly drive.

THE RIDE TO DAWSON CITY

A couple of days later I headed up the Mayo Road to my new job. The bus ride was beautiful. The weather was clear and we could see for miles, even at night.

It was about three hundred miles to Dawson City and about half way we made a pit stop at an outpost called Pelly River Crossing. There was a trading post there used by the Hudson Bay Company. Furs were still traded at Pelly River along with a few basic needs. A couple of cabins and the Trading Post made up the entire settlement.

Just before the bus landed in Pelly River some Indians had brought an old lady in on a Toboggan. The top of her head was cut and her hair was bloody and matted. Nobody seemed to know what to do so I took control and just like a doctor I ordered this and that done. I had taken a compulsory course with St. John's Ambulance when I worked in Toronto. I told the bus driver to bring the first aid kit out of the bus and told someone else to heat some water.

I took a pair of scissors and clipped the hair away from the wounds and bathed them with warm water. The wounds were at least two days old indicating that they hauled her here from quite a distance.

These people must have thought I was God. They bowed down to me. Some of them put their hand on my arm and muttered things in their native language.

It looked to me like her husband had got drunk on moose milk, then went ape and beat her up. Moose milk is an Indian brew made from herbs and roots. Its colour is white and it is said that it packs a wallop. It appeared that the man had transferred the wallop to this woman.

As we got back on the bus I told the Trading Post manager to phone Whitehorse Hospital and have a helicopter sent up. We continued on our way and the scenery was fantastic even at night. We saw moose, wolves, rabbits and ptarmigan. I landed at the job site in early afternoon and met Len Rice, the owner of the Company.

There were a total of five men plus an engineer and Len Rice in the camp. The five of us slept in a construction trailer, which was quite comfortable. The engineer and Len Rice slept in a room adjacent to the camp kitchen.

My job was crane operator at the start. Later on I acquired the rather dubious extra job of cook's helper. That job included going to the river and breaking a hole in the ice and getting a pail of water for breakfast every morning.

Here I was, breaking a hole in the ice again just as I did at our cabin in Whitehorse. We also had the cook, who became the eighth member of our crew. He was a great cook and the food was excellent, but he had a problem common among construction men. He had not yet been weaned from the bottle.

I didn't explain our job as of yet, so I'd better do it now. The town of Aklavik was beginning to sink into the permafrost, as the ice age moved north. The alternative to letting the town sink was to move it across the Mackenzie River. The new town was to be called Inuvik. There was no road to Aklavik.

Building the new town on the other side of the river made sense. The town would be on solid rock and it would be possible to build a road right to the town site. Parts of the road were now finished.

Our job was to build a bridge over the Klondike River about three miles in from the road to Dawson City. The river was only about one hundred feet wide at this point. It doesn't sound like too big a job to build a bridge this long, but in this isolation it ended up being a pretty big job. We battled for survival in the cold weather. Supplies were late getting to the job and sometimes never arrived.

We had to dig the footings down to rock and pour concrete in the hole before the river seeped in. The concrete was mixed on the site and was kept from freezing with giant heaters. Sometimes it was the men who had to be kept from freezing. When the temperature dipped to fifty below zero Fahrenheit the men were not allowed to go outside except for a few minutes to check the engines which we kept running all the time.

Big Russ said it was so cold one morning that he saw a squirrel pushing another one to get her started. It was in one of these cold snaps that Big Russ called me over to the oil tanks. He had a stick and was rolling motor oil on the stick like taffy. A tall tale? No, Big Russ told me that he still has the stick for proof. Russ was a big

Englishman from Edmonton and he had an English sense of humour. He was also as strong as an ox, hence the name Big Russ.

The bitter cold reminded me of a poem by Robert Service about the mythical "Kee Bird:"

This bird looks just like a buzzard.
It's large, it's hideous, it's bold.
At night it circles the North Pole.
Crying, "Kee, Kee, Keerist but it's cold."

It was during one of these cold snaps that our cook got into the booze and fell and cut his head up pretty bad. They wrapped him up and took him in to Dawson City to the doctor. He ended up staying there for three or four days so guess who ended up as cook? I must have done okay because nobody complained of stomachache, at least not to me. They knew better. I was ready to give that job away ASAP.

Our kitchen was fired by propane and we were in one of our cold snaps. Propane will not flow at around thirty degrees below zero Fahrenheit. One of the mornings was far below that temperature and I had to cook breakfast.

I got the guys to help me get blankets and warm them on the heaters in the bunkhouse. We then wrapped the tanks with warm blankets. About ten a.m. we had the propane in the kitchen.

I was glad when the cook got back. We made sure to keep the booze away from him after that.

Helen wrote me the odd letter up there, usually apologizing for her behaviour that night in Whitehorse.

One letter came that I couldn't quite figure out. It was from France.

I opened the letter and it was from Sue, the girl from Trenton. She had been transferred to France a while before. I didn't remember how she got my address nor did I care. I was writing her a return letter within the hour. It was great to hear from her. We started to correspond and that was a happy time for me.

ANOTHER RIDE TO REMEMBER

One of the steam Jennies that we used to keep the concrete from freezing went on the fritz. The boss found a replacement at a road construction camp about eighty miles up the new road.

The problem was that we had to go and get it. Len Rice knew the dangers of the north so he equipped one of the trucks accordingly. The truck had a winch on the front, a pile of wood in the back, about five cans of gas, some cables, ropes and heaven knows what else. In the front were a heavy sleeping bag and enough food to last a week. All this preparation to go eighty miles didn't make much sense to me.

The question arose as to who was to be the designated driver, so I volunteered.

The boss said they could do without the crane for a day, so off I went. Up through the Yukon there are hot springs and the water flows down on the roadway and freezes. It will make a vehicle slide right into the ditch. The only problem is that the "ditch" is sometimes one thousand feet deep. And then there are mirages, when you see something that is not there and, vice versa, you don't see things that are there. All in all, it makes winter driving interesting to say the least.

About halfway through the trip I hit a snow bank. I couldn't see the curve in the road and went straight into a snow bank. There are no trees up there, which is the cause of these mirages. And because there are no trees, I was unable to pull myself out with the winch.

I started out walking toward Inuvik. It was a nice day and I had no idea how far it was to the next settlement. I walked a few miles and a road gang came along in a four-wheel drive truck. We went back and pulled my truck out of the snow bank and I proceeded north. I found that there was nothing for at least forty miles. If that truck had not picked me up I probably would still be walking.

I landed at the construction camp and found that it was shut down for the winter. The only inhabitants were a watchman and his dog. What a lonely winter he must have had.

We loaded the steam generator and I headed for home. The trip was uneventful and I arrived back at our camp at two o'clock in the morning.

DAWSON CITY

We would go in to Dawson City occasionally for an evening or for a Sunday afternoon.

Dawson City had close to thirty thousand people in the gold rush days but now it's a ghost town. Hundreds of houses and businesses lie vacant as silent reminders of the gold rush days. In the 1960's the population of Dawson City was about three hundred. There were five hotels that were still operating in the town, although some of them were barely operating.

The year I was there they were restoring the town in preparation for the Dawson City Festival, which is now an annual event.

I was in the Red Feather Saloon when there were traces of gold dust in the cracks of the floor. I saw Klondike Kate's bawdyhouse before they began to restore it.

Robert Service's cabin is designated an historic site in the Yukon. I saw some of his poems still hanging on the wall.

It was interesting listening to the stories told by the old "sourdoughs" who had lived all their life in the Yukon. Some of the tales were a little tall but still interesting. They told how supplies for the boomtown of Dawson City were transported from Skagway through the Chilcoot Pass to the new town. Broken down wagons and skeletons of horses on the Trail of '98 were grim reminders of the people who didn't make it.

Although the gold rush days were long gone, the old prospectors were still panning for gold and there were gold dredges still working on Bonanza Creek. Bonanza Creek was the big strike that launched the Gold Rush in 1898.

Gold dredges are interesting machines and I took a trip to see one working. I had the satisfaction of standing in world-famous Bonanza Creek. It is about six inches deep and barely three feet across. The dredge barge was about seventy-five feet long and twenty-five feet wide and it was floating in Bonanza Creek! Was this a Yukon Tale? Not really–a little ingenuity works wonders.

The barge had a huge boom on the front that went deep down to the bedrock under the creek. That is where gold is found.

The boom would swing back and forth across the front of the barge picking up gravel. The gravel would then pass over the sluice box on the barge. Any gold was taken out, and the gravel passed over the back of the barge and back into the pool of water.

The dredge was floating but had nowhere to go until the boom dredged out in front. Then the machine would move ahead a few feet. Sometimes it moved a total of less than one mile per summer.

"Snow Monster" Dawson City, Yukon.
Yours truly between the front wheels. This snow train pulled six flat bed trailers with all wheels driving. Each trailer was fourty feet long and about 18 feet wide. It had a crew of six who lived in the huge engine cab. They carried supplies, fuel, lumber, machinery, etc. to all the far northern outposts between Fairbanks, Alaska and Yellowknife, N.W.T. It made one trip across and back each winter.

OOPS!

One day while working on the bridge structure I slipped and fell to the ice below. It was only about ten feet but I twisted my back. They sent me to Whitehorse and I went to a chiropractor. The chiropractor was a lady and it was nice having her fuss over me, poking me here and there. I was glad when she told me to come back the next day. The next day she had my back almost as good as new. She was cute and I was disappointed when she told me I didn't need to come back unless it bothered me again. I left Whitehorse and returned to work. A couple of months later we finished the job.

We loaded a lot of equipment on the two light trucks and headed down the line.

When we reached Whitehorse I decided to stay overnight and renew old acquaintances and say my good-byes to Helen. She heard I was in town so she bought a new dress to go out the following night. I had Russ with me and we couldn't stay another night. When I told Helen this, it opened the floodgates. I felt like a louse but I just had to go.

We stayed in Watson Lake the second night, close to the BC border.

A girl I knew from Whitehorse was working in the bar in Watson Lake. She said she was leaving for Edmonton in a couple of days and I should look her up when I was in Edmonton.

Big Russ, the guy that was riding with me, called me a stud with girls at every stop.

We started down the Alaska Highway, headed for Edmonton, and if you have ever travelled the Alaska Highway you will know what they mean when they say:

Winding in and winding out
Fills my mind with serious doubt
As to whether the dudes that built this route
Were going to hell or coming out!

We got to Edmonton and got our termination slips. I boarded a train headed for Toronto. The Yukon experience was now history.

KEENE

I came home from the Yukon and landed a job with a construction company from Guelph called Cox Construction.

They sent me to a job in Keene, Ontario, which is near Peterborough, which ironically became my home a few years later and still is today.

Since I had been working in remote areas, I didn't have a car. This prompted me to go into Peterborough to shop for one. I settled on a beautiful Oldsmobile 88. It was a 1958, which was nearly new, and the price was twelve hundred dollars. I put two hundred down and financed a thousand. That car was a prime example of the saying "beauty is only skin deep."

On the way back to Keene from Peterborough, a distance of about eight miles, I saw fire coming from under the instrument panel and the smoke was choking me. I shut the motor off and the next day they towed it back to Peterborough. The dealer was very good about the whole thing, and repaired it free of charge. I had no more trouble for about thirty days, which was the length of the warranty.

The warranty expired and shortly after all hell let loose. The carburetor went, and the fuel pump quit. I had to put on a new radiator and the list goes on.

About that time I had planned a trip to Europe, mainly to see Sue. The transmission went on the car and the bill was over three hundred dollars. That pretty well ended any hope of a trip to Europe.

The highway job in Keene came to an end in the fall and my car had eaten up any money that I made and more.

I had to find a job real soon so I hired on with a Company in Kitchener called Kieswetter Excavating. Kitchener is a German settlement populated with fine, fun loving and open-minded people.

Kieswetter did a lot of sewer and water main construction. We built new sewer systems and I enjoyed the work. Art Carney would have liked this kind of sewer job. Inevitably we acquired the name of "sewer rats."

I had just purchased a boat and motor a short time before I went to the Yukon. It was an ideal boat for water skiing. I really got into water skiing in Kitchener with some buddies. We burned more gas in my boat than I burned in my car, which was easy because the damned car was in the garage half the time. What I saved in gas I spent in repairs. Even with the car acting up all the time we still had a great summer.

The Oldsmobile continued to be a drain on my pocket book. The problem was that at this time it was not in running condition. The transmission was gone again and I needed a car.

I walked a few blocks from where I lived and dropped into the Studebaker dealer's showroom. I told the boss my plight. A new '63 Studebaker Commander was just under three thousand dollars. He took the Olds as a trade in, and I added some extra cash and financed the rest. The low down payment made the payments steep but at least I had a new car. The Studebaker turned out to be a super car so I was back on the road again, until a short time later, when I ended up in the air again.

THE BAHAMA DRAMA

That fall I met a friend who had just arrived home from Grand Bahama. He didn't paint a very rosy picture of the Bahamas. It probably stemmed from the fact that it was his first time away from home. A little homesickness probably made things look worse than they actually were.

My staff car. A Triumph Herald. West End, Grand Bahama

I decided that the Bahamas couldn't be as bad as all that. There was only one way to find out and that was to see it first hand.

I heard that C.A. Pitts Construction had a job in a cement mine on Grand Bahama. I went to Pitts' office in Toronto to get more information and learned that the job was handled from the US office.

The personnel manager said that since I had worked for Pitts before he would give me a letter of recommendation. I purposely neglected to tell him that I had been fired from Pitts on the railroad job in Port Cartier, Quebec. With this recommendation in my hand I went to see my boss at Kieswetter.

I knew that business slowed down in winter so I asked for a few months off. My boss was quite agreeable.

With the recommendation from Pitts in my hand, I bought a return air ticket to Grand Bahama. If this letter didn't work I had my passage home. The letter didn't get a chance to work and I didn't use the return ticket. Fasten your seat belts. We are about to embark on another exciting adventure.

It was a bitterly cold night just after New Years when I boarded the plane for Tampa. That was my last ride in a Lockheed Super Constellation. They took them out of the skies shortly after that. What rough, noisy aircraft they were!

130

I landed in Tampa and the temperature was 80 degrees Fahrenheit. I was dressed in my winter clothes so I headed for the nearest washroom with my suitcase.

I boarded a Bahama Air Lines plane for Grand Bahama and landed about 4 p.m. just ahead of a hurricane. It was ripping up trees and it tore the roof off a powerhouse just by the airport. The fire was flying in all directions and the lights went out in the airport. This was my first impression of a tropical Island. The storm lasted about one half hour and then the sun came out.

I got a taxi to take me to a hotel. Lesson number one: Do not use Bahama's taxis unless absolutely necessary. The driver took off out of there with tires squealing and went around a blind curve on the left-hand side of the road. I nearly died until I realized that this is the side of the road they drive on in the Bahamas.

He pulled up at the Diamond Head Hotel just about a mile from the airport. It was a small hotel three stories high with about twenty rooms and was owned by a Canadian. I decided to get a room there. About eighteen hours before this I was in Malton Airport and it was cold. I guess that was why I appreciated this place so much.

I had a beautiful room with glass windows top to bottom and about twenty feet away the sea was gently lapping at the beach. I plunked my old travel companion in a corner and we were home for at least one night.

In my mind this was as good as it gets. I walked on the beach and I could hear the island music in a nearby bar. I wanted to share this enchantment with someone but I was all alone.

I went downstairs to the nightclub located right in the hotel and ended up having a beer and talking to the Canadian who owned the place. I found out he was from the Ottawa area. I didn't know anyone from up there and he didn't know anything about the Collingwood area so we just talked. When I went to bed, I slept soundly in my room by the sea.

The next morning I found out where the cement mine was and hitchhiked toward it. No more taxis! An American picked me up in a beat up station wagon and I found out that he was going directly to the cement plant. Lucky me. My first impression of the cement plant was made right at the gate. Dusty!

I found the office and went in. There was dust on the doorknob, dust on the windowsills and dust on the chairs. I would have had to wipe the dust off the chair to sit down but I didn't. I just turned around and walked out. I decided that I wasn't ready to die yet with my lungs full of cement dust.

It was a nice day so I started walking up the road toward the Diamond Head Hotel at West End. What a terrible road! I had a problem dodging the potholes and I was walking. Some of those potholes would tear a wheel off a car.

It was a beautiful morning so I just walked along looking at the exotic new world in which I was living. There were strange trees and shrubs–palms, palmettos etc. Land crabs scurried across the road in front of me. Little salamanders darted here and there.

When I reached the main road it was really warm. The southern sun was beating down and it was a long way to West End so I broke the rule and flagged a taxi. This guy wasn't quite as bad. "Where y' all wanna go Mon?" he asked. I told him "the Diamond Head Hotel."

We got to the hotel and I took time to count my money and to write a letter to Sue in France. I didn't have to be a rocket scientist to see my money wasn't going to last long down here. Things were expensive.

I went to the Canadian who operated the hotel and got him to give me a run down on the area. He told me that there was a small construction company just up the street. The name of the company was West End Construction. I decided to eat first and check out the company later.

There was a little restaurant and bar right beside the hotel. It seemed every building on this street was a bar.

I went into the restaurant and ordered conch chowder. Well, that conch chowder had to be at least half chili peppers. I was like a fiery dragon. These Bahamians sure love their chili and jalapeno peppers.

The next morning I went in the same little place for breakfast, and as I probably would do anywhere else I ordered bacon and eggs. I thought

My weekly tab at a local restaurant in the West End. Note my name at the top.

the little black guy would fall down laughing. "Bacon and eggs, Mon? What the hell is dat?" I found out that the usual breakfast in the Bahamas is boiled fish and grits. I always like to try new and crazy foods so I ordered "boiled fish and grits." Again it was loaded with peppers and my tongue was hanging halfway to my knees. How was I going to get a decent meal down here?

After breakfast I went up to West End Construction. It was only a ten-minute walk from the hotel to the construction yard. When I got there I was told that the two owners were in Trinidad looking at a job and wouldn't be back for a few days.

I went back to the hotel. I loved it and even by today's standards it would be right up there at the top. For the next few days I just tried to get my bearings of the area.

There was a new Jack Tar Resort being built just outside the village of West End and I noticed that West End Construction was doing some work on the project. It looked like they had lots of work down here, but what really impressed me was the fact that they were in Trinidad bidding on work. With this Company I would have a chance to see other islands.

The two owners landed back home from Trinidad a few days later and I got to talk to one of them. His name was Sonny Waugh. He was white but was born and raised on Grand Bahama. His partner was Juan Fernandez, a Mexican who came to Grand Bahama as a child.

Sonny took me in a back room, which was supposed to be his office. I said that I was a Canadian and I was looking for work. The Canadian in the Diamond Head told me to explain that I was Canadian because Canadians were well liked in the Bahamas. I mentioned some of my construction experience and had a whole line to tell him but I didn't get a chance.

"When can y'all start work?" he asked. I said I could start in the morning. I had been in his office all of two minutes and I had a job.

He said my salary would be fifty pounds a week, a figure that I considered pretty good. It was equal to about one hundred and fifty dollars Canadian. He also gave me a car to drive because before I left his office he had promoted me to a general supervisor.

Things were happening almost too fast for me. I had assumed quite a responsibility and was determined not to screw up.

The men who worked for me were all native Bahamians except three or four Haitians who did the basic jobs. We had a bulldozer and two motor scrapers working on the east end of the island at Lucaya.

The Lucayan Beach Hotel would be the biggest gambling casino in the Western Hemisphere when it was completed.

Our company had the job of grading the area and building roads for the proposed subdivision. We also had a bulldozer doing small clearing jobs around the island.

I was now a workingman but I couldn't afford to stay at the Diamond Head much longer.

I moved to a rather modest place down the road in a settlement called The Bight. Kenny was a native Bahamian and he had this little business of his own. Downstairs was a bar and restaurant and upstairs there were about eight rustic rooms.

I paid three pounds a week for my room. Meals in the restaurant were about one dollar per meal. I now was able to have money for clothes and a little nightlife.

Things were pretty good, except at first I had trouble sleeping because my room was over the bar and the noise went on almost all night. There was no curfew on bars. They could stay open as long as they had customers. My room was not exactly soundproof. I could see light from the bar through the cracks in the floor, but what the heck, that's what you get for three pounds a week.

I wasn't very long getting settled. I had a job, a car and a place to live in a beautiful island in the West Indies.

It was good to sleep in on Sundays with the southern sun shining in my window. I would listen to the Caribbean music on my bedside radio. Little salamanders would dart around on the walls and ceiling.

The southern nights are almost the same temperature as the daytime, and I didn't have air conditioning. I remember one particular night, when it was too warm to sleep, I grabbed my blanket and went across the road to the ocean and curled up on a jetty.

In the morning one of the locals came by and saw me. "Hey Mon!" he said, "There are scorpions around here and they like to hide under a jetty like this one."

He proceeded to look for scorpions, and to my relief he came up empty handed. Scorpions are active at night and they hide in the daytime. He told me that scorpions like to hide in shoes: "Y'all better shake yo' shoes out every mawnin'."

134

I didn't need to be told twice. It was a habit I developed, and I found myself checking my shoes after I came back to Canada a few months later.

Things were totally different on this job from what I was used to in Canada.

First of all, the island life is a lot slower and more laid back. My employees were frustrating. They were late for work, took extra long lunch hours, and at times I would find some of them sleeping under a palm tree. I soon found out that if I fired one of them I ended up doing his job. It was hard to find anyone who wanted to work.

One job we had was on a remote part of the island, so I picked the crew up each morning in my car. I was instructed to pick Paul up first and then go back and get the other men. If I picked Paul up last he would be drunk. It was easy to tell when Paul was drunk. His felt hat would be slid way back on his head. If I came to Paul's place and his hat was on the back of his head I just kept right on going. I remember one morning I came for Paul and he was not at the roadside waiting. I blew the horn and soon he appeared, but he was not alone. His wife, a big hefty Mulatto had him by the ear as she marched him right up to my car cussing about him being drunk all the time. As we drove away Paul looked back and mumbled "Mammy is old grouch, Mon." Paul was a good grader operator once I got him on the job.

Mostly the men were pretty good workers after they taught me how to handle them. Even then they sometimes made things interesting for me...make that frustrating.

I found the food unusually spicy as I mentioned earlier, so I decided to get the cook in the Diamond Head to make me up a good old Canadian steak one evening. After an unusually long wait this cute little black waitress came out of the kitchen with my steak order.

There was a problem—her favourite song was playing, so she just sat my steak on top of the jukebox and started dancing with a guy who was hanging around.

I was about ready to hit the roof when I suddenly remembered that I was an alien here. Considering discretion to be the better part of valour I settled down and waited, and waited, and mumbled to myself.

135

When the song was completely over the waitress picked up my plate, and still dancing and skipping along she delivered it to my table. It was as cold as an Eskimo's nose but I wouldn't dare let her take it back to warm it. Lord no! I waited long enough to get it. I wasn't about to wait another half hour.

About a month or two later I was in a bar in West End, and the beer was sliding down pretty good. I looked down the bar and there was the waitress who served me in the Diamond Head. She was nursing a Creme de Cacao and cream, a popular drink down there.

After a few more beers I looked around and the girl and I were the only two at the bar, so I decided to introduce myself. I slid over to the stool next to her and after a minute or two I offered, "Buy you a drink?" She looked at me and without a word she nodded yes, which meant, "Yeah, okay sucker."

I had put down a few beers by now and so I decided to start a conversation. I don't remember what I said but I remember that I was the only one talking. Finally amid my babbling I said: "You know I really like you coloured people." She took a look at me and uttered her first words of the evening. "Mon, Ah is not coloured, ah is just plain black."

I really liked my job aside from frustrations caused by my lackadaisical employees. I just decided that it was a way of life in the warm country, so I adopted the old saying, "If you can't beat them, join them."

It was a good life. On Sundays I would go for a drive around the island, or swim at one of the beaches. Sometimes I would go fishing with one of the natives.

Kenny, my landlord at The Bight, was an avid fisherman, and I liked to go out in his dory with him. We would catch green turtles, southern lobster, sea crabs, a variety of pan fish, red snappers, sheepshead, sailor's choice and many more with names I no longer remember.

What I remember most was how he caught lobster. The lobster of the Caribbean is more like a crawfish. They weigh up to a pound and are excellent tasting.

When we went after lobster we had two long poles. One had a bent wire on the end and the other one had a net. The one with the wire was called a teaser.

Kenny would spot a lobster on the bottom in about eight feet of water. He would tease the lobster until it sprang up off the seabed. Immediately he slipped the net under it and we had a live lobster in the boat. Kenny caught a lot of these each morning. He would sell them to the people waiting at his dock. Everyone knew Kenny would have a catch of something from the sea.

My job was interesting. It was more of a learning process than a job. I had to learn a whole new way of life. Like the day my boss called me into his office. My first thought was that I was probably about to be fired, but I didn't know why. He sat behind his desk and glanced out the window and then he looked me straight in the eye as he tapped the desk with his pencil. "Oh boy," I thought. "Here goes."

He looked at me for a few seconds, which seemed like an hour, before he spoke. He said "Ivan we are quite impressed with your work here so we are giving you an assignment." At least it looked like I had a job for a few more days.

THE TRINIDAD TYCOON

He tapped the desk with his pencil and he told me that a certain Mr. Tucker from Trinidad was coming to Grand Bahama where he had a holiday cottage. Some cottage! It looked more like the Taj Mahal. I learned that Mr. Tucker owned a large plantation in Trinidad and that was where my bosses were when I had to wait for them to come home before I was hired.

Mr. Tucker was a poor man probably only worth a paltry ten million "Canadian" or so. If this was his cottage, I would have liked to see his house in Trinidad. He also owned a yacht that I would estimate at measuring well over two hundred feet long. He kept a crew of seven on the yacht year round. I was told that he grew bananas and pineapples on his plantation in Trinidad.

Anyway, getting back to my assignment, my boss Sonny went on to tell me a little about Mr. Tucker. He mentioned that Mr. Tucker was about to contract a huge job at the "cottage" on Grand Bahama. He said that from watching me he had decided that I was more suited to talk to Mr. Tucker about a large contract like this. Sonny showed me a plan of the proposed contract. It entailed building a canal from the ocean to a proposed turning basin behind the estate, big enough to turn his yacht. The sea can get pretty rough on that side of the island so the basin would afford protection for the yacht.

Sonny told me that I had a breakfast meeting reserved at the Caravelle Club in a few days. In the meantime I was to go to the Club and be fitted for a tuxedo that I was to wear for my meeting with Mr. Tucker.

I was excited but I was also intimidated by the grandeur of the Caravelle Club. I had never seen anything like it in my life, and I was on my best behaviour on the morning that we were to have the meeting.

I got dressed in the monkey suit right there at the Club. I felt like a fish out of water in that suit as I prepared to meet Mr. Tucker. But then I thought, "What the hell, if I screw up I have a return ticket to Canada in my room."

I went to the desk and said I was supposed to meet Mr. Tucker. They went and told him and in a few minutes he arrived at the

138

front desk. We introduced ourselves and right away I felt comfortable with the man.

The people at the front desk were fussing over him and bending over backwards to do things for him.

I thought, "Geez, maybe this guy owns the Caravelle as well." We were escorted to a table and I have to say this was no ordinary table.

The maitre d' took us into the courtyard, which had palm trees all around. The tables were built around the trees and we sat at one of these tables with a palm growing up through the centre of the table.

The walkways were marble slabs. Scantily clad cigarette girls walked among the tables while "breakfast" was being served, which wasn't the kind of breakfast that I knew back home. No bacon and eggs and coffee served here. They served caviar and croissants. The waitress put down a cup and saucer by our plates and I assumed it was either tea or coffee. Man, was I in for a surprise! It was cognac and some tropical juice served in a teacup.

I had to pinch myself to see if I was dreaming. Here I am a country boy raised in a log cabin up in Canada and look at me now. The Queen would have marvelled at this place.

It was not long until we got down to business and I could see I was dealing with a shrewd businessman. My only weapon against him was B.S. and I guess I laid it on pretty thick.

Near the end of our conversation he reached over and shook my hand. "Young man" he said. "You seem to know what you are talking about. We will be in touch." I was glad to say my good-byes to Mr. Tucker but I was especially glad to get out of that hot monkey suit.

I got in my car and headed off in the general direction of West End, happy to be free again on the beautiful island of Grand Bahama.

Things were mostly routine for the next few days. I was enjoying the weather, no shirt every day and just enjoying the February sun.

One day I was sitting in my car in Lucaya watching our machinery working on the proposed parking lot for the new Casino. I looked around and there was my boss pulling up beside me. "Oh shit," I thought, "what did I do now?"

He came around his car and reached out his hand for a handshake. In his best Bahamian drawl he said "Mon, y'all must 'a had a good meeting with Mr. Tucker. We got the contract!"

I decided to celebrate by dropping into a bar on the way home. The "bar" I chose was a plywood shack about ten feet square. It had a jukebox, a counter about three feet long, and an antique refrigerator in the corner. A half dozen liquor bottles sat on a makeshift shelf behind the counter. It had a couple of boxes on the floor if I wanted to sit down. This about completely describes the interior of this so-called bar.

There were three other people in there, along with the guy behind the bar, at the time I arrived.

One fellow was playing the same song over and over on the jukebox. Finally the other man, who had his woman with him, went over and shut the jukebox off. They had been drinking and a fight ensued. They went outside and the woman took off her spike-heeled shoe and brought it down on the other man's head. The spike went deep in the top of his head. He died on the spot. I left a vapour trail getting out of that place. I wasn't about to be a witness to a murder.

It had been quite a day! The good news from my boss and it had to be screwed up by a thing like this.

The Bahamian winter wore on and I enjoyed the beautiful sunshine. The sun shone just about every day and the stars were amazing at night.

We started the big job for Mr. Tucker. It involved underwater blasting, as most of the island was coral rock. When we blasted, dozens of dead fish came to the surface. This attracted sharks and it was a danger to the men diving to load underwater drill holes with dynamite.

If a shark became a problem these guys had the perfect solution. They would take one of the dead fish and put a dynamite cap inside of its mouth. A long wire was attached to the explosive. They then threw the fish out near the shark. As soon as the shark took the fish in its mouth they touched the wires to a battery. Pop! And the shark almost lost his head. These guys knew all the tricks including how to trick me, their boss.

I would go down to the job at Lucaya. A couple of hours later I would come back and there was no one to be seen, and the workboat was gone. They were fishing around the point out of my sight.

I could hardly blame them. It was too hot to work anyway. About this time my boss landed another big job. This one was exciting. The contract called for us to build seven small airstrips on seven of the out islands.

Bahama Airways was organizing a tour for people to land on these islands. They named it the "Hedge Hopping Tour."

Most of these islands were primitive and sparsely inhabited. There was Little Abaco, Eleuthera, San Salvador, Mayaguana, Cat Kay, and a couple of others as well.

San Salvador and Mayaguana airstrips were to be my assignment. My boss looked after the others.

I was finally going to see San Salvador, the famous island where Columbus allegedly first touched the New World. I had read about San Salvador in history books in school. They said that there was a monument to Columbus on the Island. Boy, was I in for a surprise! About the only thing on that Island was the Columbus Monument. The rest was just a giant rock jutting up out of the Caribbean with a population of about twenty. I got a crew started on the proposed airstrip and I headed home to Grand Bahama in the Company plane, a four-seater Cessna.

From our headquarters on Grand Bahama to Mayaguana was about three days by barge. We loaded a barge with a grader, tractor and scraper, a bulldozer and a few accessories as well as fuel. I stayed on the home Island for a couple of days and checked over the jobs in progress.

On the third day I took the plane down to Mayaguana. I was amazed at how the pilot could land in such a small area. It was about five o'clock when he took off and I was on my own. A barefoot boy who was about twelve years old showed me to my room.

My "room" was a plywood cabin about eight feet square. There were no windows, just a door and a mattress in the corner.

I took a quick check of the immediate area. There seemed to be someone behind every tree looking out at me. My boss had prearranged meals for me because there was no restaurant. I ate at a nearby house and the food was not bad, but they had no table so I ate standing up.

It was about six p.m. and still daylight. I didn't have a car, which didn't matter—there were no roads. I decided that I might as well work so I took the dozer and started ripping up the coral rock that would be used later to build the airstrip. I worked for a couple of hours and by then it was dark.

I could see the island people silhouetted on a small hill close by. I had my doubts about whether the wheel had yet been invented on Mayaguana or San Salvador. I shut the machine down and checked it over.

The natives came down from the hill and the women had these little baskets made from palmetto fronds. They gave the baskets to me and I found them to be full of yams, limes, lemons, bananas and other tropical fruit.

They must have given me twelve baskets. I thanked them, but what was I to do with all of this stuff? I ate a couple of bananas and when they all went home I had to throw the stuff in the mangrove thicket.

I had no way of cooking in my cabin. I was only there a couple of days to give the men instructions and then I flew back to Grand Bahama.

EXTRACURRICULAR ACTIVITIES

By some stroke of fate I made friends with a rather cute Haitian girl named Yvose. She knew very little English because her language was Creole, a mixture of Spanish and French. I spoke to her in French and we managed to understand each other reasonably well.

"Papa Doc" Duvalier ruled Haiti in the sixties. He was a ruthless dictator and was the reason that there were so many Haitian refugees in the islands of the Caribbean.

I had a strange relationship with "Eve." (I had a problem pronouncing her real name). Because of the poverty and abuse that she was subjected to in Haiti, I sort of became her Santa Claus.

She had never had shoes on her feet until she was about sixteen. She had never owned a piece of Haitian money in her life.

It was interesting teaching her about the real world outside of Haiti.

Her hut was about a five-minute walk from my place so we used to get together often. Mainly we were trying to learn each other's language.

I gave her some money one time to buy some food because there was no food at her place. Through sign language etc. she insisted that I come to her place for dinner that night. I looked around her place and all she had to cook on was a kerosene-stove. A few plastic dishes were on a shelf. But the place was clean.

I wondered what kind of dinner I was in for, but I was in for a surprise. The food was great and I couldn't believe that she cooked it on that little kerosene stove. My plate of food was almost covered with sliced tomatoes. I like tomatoes but this was rather much.

She didn't sit with me to eat. She stood beside me and my plate was the only thing on the table. Two or three times after this I was invited for dinner and each time I happily accepted. Each time she put my plate on the table and stood beside me while I ate. Each time my plate was covered with sliced tomatoes.

I couldn't believe all the tomatoes she was putting on my plate so I asked her "Why the tomatoes?" She laughed and told me in broken English that she asked some friends what a Canadian liked best for food. One of them said that they heard Canadians ate a lot of tomatoes. I tried not to laugh as I told her to just cook the Haitian way.

I think I only ate there once after that. There were no tomatoes. It was about this time that I decided to move from The Bight to a cabin on the company property up in West End

The cabin didn't exactly rate five stars but what the heck, it had a bed and a dresser and it was free— compliments of my bosses. Eve's cabin was about halfway between my old place and my new place in West End.

Eve would sometimes get depressed and worry about her family back in Haiti. I remember one night I was in bed in my cabin in West End and Eve came in. She sat down on the edge of my bed and was crying. She said she wondered if her family was still alive back in Haiti. I tried to comfort her but I was pretty awkward, coming from an all-male family, so I told her to lie down and spend the night. She was soon asleep.

A few days later I dropped by her place after I had a couple of payday drinks with the gang. I ended up eating there, which was the time there were no tomatoes.

She said that she was lonesome and wanted me to stay and keep her company for a little while. I told her I had to go because the boys were waiting for me at the Diamond Head Bar.

I went down the street to the Bar and sat down with the crew. There were four of us so I ordered four drinks. I took out my wallet to pay for the drinks and there was only a one pound note left of my pay.

My first thought was: "That little bitch stole my money."

I excused myself and walked to Eve's place. I was raging mad when she met me at the door smiling. She handed me the rest of my pay cheque at the same time blasting me for spending my money. I was so glad to get my money back that I gave her some of it, and to boot I stayed with her and we talked and talked. She told me I was her only friend on the island, and I believed that to be true.

The next day I bought her a short wave radio so she could get news from Haiti. I don't think I ever saw anyone as happy as she was that day. That radio went with her everywhere. She came and gave me a big hug and cried on my shoulder. No one had ever been this good to her in her life.

144

I dropped in a day or so later and she was very sick. I didn't know what the heck was the matter. I figured it was some tropical disease or something. I was unable to care for her because I was working every day. She said she had some friends in Nassau, and I knew there was a good hospital there, so I loaded her on a cargo boat headed for Nassau. The last I saw her she was waving to me, and the radio was tightly held under her arm.

Every day I went to the Post Office hoping for a letter from France. I was excited every time I got a letter. Sue was my number one interest, and these other relationships were more like friendships.

Little did I know the day I went to Trenton to see Sue that sooner or later my life would change forever.

I became friends with Jack Hamilton who was the owner of a small airline on Grand Bahama. He flew passengers and freight around the Bahama Islands and Fort Lauderdale, Florida.

Every Saturday he had a flight to Bimini where he stayed over and came back Sunday. He let me come along with him a couple of times.

There are few, if any, places in the world as enchanting as the Island of Bimini. It is a very small Island about sixty miles off the coast of Florida in the Fort Lauderdale area.

We landed there about five p.m. and it was dark about six thirty, which is when the island came to life. The main road had shops on both sides where soft music played and dim lights were all around.

The shops had no doors because they never closed. They had beads hanging down in the doorways and the people were friendly. What a beautiful place! I walked on the beach alone wishing I had someone to walk with.

INDEPENDENCE DAY

About two months after I arrived in the Bahamas it became an independent country and was no longer under British rule.

The day it became independent was cause for a celebration. The way these people celebrated was frightening. They broke shop windows and smashed full bottles of rum on the street. They even upset a car on the street, which happened to be my car, a Triumph Herald.

A very short time after Independence Day the boxing world saw Cassius Clay and Sonny Liston in a championship fight. As we know Clay won and this was cause for another celebration, which ended up nothing short of a riot. These people seemed to have no self-control when it came to celebrations.

Nothing much out of the ordinary happened in the next few months. I was enjoying my job and the weather was super. I also enjoyed Sue's letters from France.

I was working in the Bahamas without a work visa, which was illegal, but because of complications back in Canada I was unable to acquire a visa. The immigration department started to get on my case but my boss kept giving them a bum steer.

It was about this time that I received a letter from Sue saying that she was coming home from France.

The authorities were getting pretty hot on my tail so about a day or so later I headed for the airport with the Immigration guys right behind me.

I landed back in Kitchener, picked up my car and renewed acquaintances with a few friends before starting back on my old job.

HOME AT LAST

That weekend I went to Fort Erie to see Sue who came home a few days prior to my return.

On my weekend visits to the Rasch house things started to heat up. Cupid's arrow went deep.

I was beginning to think it was time to

My toys of the sixties.
One red, one blonde. The blonde prevailed.

leave my rowdy friends and to change my wild and crazy way of life and put the old suitcase on the shelf. Besides, I was beginning to get a little long in the tooth. It was time for me to begin a normal life.

A short time later Sue got a job in Kitchener and not long after that she became a March bride.

Shortly after I came home I purchased a little Triumph TR-2 sports car. It needed some work so I did most of the restoration in my spare time. We had some good times in the summer in the little sports car.

When we got married I sold the TR-2 and we used the money for a honeymoon in Florida.

We travelled off the main roads and most of the time we were lost, but we didn't care. Food and lodging was cheap and the friendly people kept steering us in the right direction. We finally made it to Miami.

We had not reserved any lodging in Miami so we ended up in a fleabag motel on Miami Beach the first night.

In the morning I phoned a man from Kitchener who owned a motel in Miami. He came and escorted us back to his motel. I think it was the first time that we weren't lost since we left the Canadian border.

147

He owned a nice little motel in the heart of Miami close to a beautiful park on the ocean. Since he knew us, he gave us a suite for half price.

He also gave us tours all over the Miami area, a clever trick on his part. His wife had to clean the motel rooms while he toured us around Miami.

Shortly after we arrived, a tornado swept across northern Florida and we got the tail winds from it in Miami. The next day we were stretched out on the beach and fell asleep. Between the wind from the storm and the hot Florida sun my chest and stomach were red and burning like hellfire.

Mr. Smith, the motel owner, came to the rescue with a jug of vinegar. It gave me relief but the smell was, well, whatever vinegar smells like.

A day or two later I decided to show my new bride how the natives in the Bahamas shinnied up a tree to get coconuts. I got a few feet up and slipped. I slid down the tree with my sunburned belly against the rough bark. Here I was on my honeymoon with a sunburned and scraped belly that even I couldn't touch.

We got back to Kitchener, which was now our home. We both had decent jobs and life was about as good as it gets.

We didn't have a lot of money but we bought a tent and went camping on weekends. We went out to dinner once in a while with friends and everything was great.

The tie that binds.

NOW WE ARE THREE

A few months later Sue happened to mention that it looked like we would soon be a family of three. It appeared that my sunburn must have healed.

We moved to a larger apartment with two bedrooms. It would be needed for obvious reasons.

One Saturday night a few months later we went out to dinner with another couple. We just finished our dinner and things began to happen with Sue, so we rushed to the hospital.

I waited in the waiting room of St. Mary's Hospital until seven a.m. and still no baby, so I decided to go home and have a shower and shave.

I wearily sat down on the sofa at home. I guess I instantly fell asleep. I woke up at nine a.m. to the phone ringing. The nurse on the other end said: "Congratulations you are the father of a baby daughter."

Damn! I spent over nine hours at the hospital and missed the whole thing anyway.

Now, with Baby Pamela, Sue had to take time off work. This reduced our income considerably.

We got a job as caretakers of a twenty-three-suite apartment building. Our caretakers' wages covered the apartment rent. It was good because Sue could work right at home.

The Property Management Company got the contract to manage a new high-rise luxury complex. It had about one hundred suites plus penthouses on the top floor.

We were asked if we would be interested in managing this new complex. After we saw the apartment that we would be living in, we decided to give it a try.

The manager's suite was beautiful, three spacious bedrooms with huge walk in closets, two bathrooms, a huge kitchen, and a large balcony.

We were now managers of Stanley Park Place.

We ended up having some problems with a few unruly tenants that we later had to evict, but the rest of the tenants were great and we had some good times together.

OUR COTTAGE

When Pam was about a year old we purchased a lakefront property in the Haliburton Highlands.

Pam loved the water. She always had to have her "baby soup" on to go swimming, but as soon as it got wet, off it came. Rumour has it that she has since learned to tolerate a wet swimsuit.

We had some good times cooking on a campfire and sleeping in the tent, although the tent caused some concern with the baby because there were forest animals around. We built a cabin eight by eight feet to sleep in, which gave us peace of mind.

My boss had some lumber neatly piled in one of the Company's gravel pits in Kitchener.

It was just perfect to build the substructure of the cottage. I asked Harold Kieswetter how much he wanted for the lumber. "Oh" He said. "Just take it and we'll talk about it later." I don't know what he meant by later because I got the lumber over thirty years ago and Harold has been dead for at least twenty. I never heard about it again.

I built the substructure on weekends and now I was ready for the sub floor. I still had no extra money so I just planned on leaving it until I got some spare cash.

FROM KITCHENER TO MISSISSAUGA

In order to keep up with the times, Kieswetter decided to downsize. This meant a layoff of about half of the employee work force, which numbered about seventy men. Most of these men were born and grew up in Kitchener and were not happy about having to relocate.

About this time my brothers needed an operator in their excavating business in Toronto. I went to my boss at Kieswetter and told him that I had another job to go to, so he could keep one of the locals in my place. This change of jobs meant we would be leaving Stanley Park Place.

When the tenants got word that we would be leaving they decided to give us a going away party. It was an emotional time for us.

One day I stepped out into the hallway and in the middle of the floor were four or five preschoolers and Pam was in the centre. They were giving her a going away present, a box of Smarties. It was enough to make a grown man cry, which I did.

Our going away party with the tenants was on a much higher scale but was very emotional as well. That party lasted for three days and nights! We were only there for day one, so we missed most of the celebration.

I moved my family to Mississauga and worked with my brothers for a couple of years, but I really wasn't happy with the job.

I got a job with Cliffside Pipelayers, a Company that laid gas pipe for Consumers Gas. I really liked this job and the pay was excellent.

CATCHING A THIEF

One day I was doing a trenching job to supply gas to a new housing development that was under construction in Brampton. As the day wore on I noticed one of the workers was carrying panels of plywood out to the back and hiding them in the long grass. This went on all afternoon and the wheels in my head were beginning to turn.

He was stealing this plywood and would be back after dark to pick it up.

I decided to hang around after I was finished work. When everyone was gone, I drove over to where I saw him put the plywood. I loaded it all in my station wagon. All sixteen sheets of sub floor plywood. That was exactly the amount I needed for the cottage sub floor. My car was loaded down until the tires were touching the fenders but I didn't feel bad, I was stealing from a thief! So I installed the sub floor.

I gathered up some two by four studs that had been used for concrete forms. They had done their job as concrete forms but they were still good for wall studs.

Now it was time for windows. I was doing an excavating job sometime later for a homeowner. I noticed that he had two huge plate glass windows leaning against a tree in the back yard. I asked him how much he wanted for the windows.

"Oh!" he said, "I've been trying to get rid of them. Just throw them in your truck when you leave."

Those two windows gave our cottage a huge glass front facing the lake.

Up until now my total expenses were a few pounds of nails and two or three bags of cement.

My luck had run out as far as freebees went, so we bought some material and closed the cottage in and installed the roof.

At this time Sue was nine months pregnant. I left her at home with her sister, who had agreed to stay at our house with Sue just in case, and went up to work on the cottage. I had made arrangements sometime before with a friend to help me install the floor that weekend. We had done considerable work that day so we were tired and crawled into our sleeping bags early.

At about two a.m. there was a knock at the door. I awoke from a sound sleep only to meet an OPP officer at the door. A million thoughts went through my mind. How did he find me up here in the backwoods? Something must be wrong at home.

The officer smiled and said: "Congratulations! You are the father of a baby boy." An over-exuberant sister-in-law had persuaded the cops to find me to tell me the good news.

It had taken about two years to build the cottage. We had many good times there during its construction and after it was finished as well. We had installed a Franklin fireplace and also some electric heat so we went up occasionally in the winter. But there was a problem. We had a fine cottage but we didn't own a house. Our family needed a yard to play in.

We decided to sell the cottage and with the money we bought a house in a nice neighbourhood in Bramalea, now Brampton.

We were now owners of a piece of urban real estate. Given the fact that Sue and I were both raised in country settings we had some adjustments to make.

About a year-and-a-half after buying our house in Bramalea, Pitts Construction bought out my employers, Cliffside Pipelayers. As the new company restructured I began to wonder if I was going to be told to "Close the door from the outside."

By now our house had risen in value considerably so we decided to sell it.

We thought Peterborough would be a nice place to live and raise the kids.

PETERBOROUGH

We decided on a partially finished larger house in Fairbairn Meadows, a subdivision on the outskirts of Peterborough. It had a large lot, over one acre in size, so the kids now had room to roam.

We moved into an apartment in Bramalea until we finished building our new house.

Autum brilliance in Peterborough

Suddenly one day, as I was working on the house, it struck me. We had no income and things were getting critical financially.

I went to work at the job I knew best, operating an excavator for a local company. The wages were considerably less than I was accustomed to with the Pipeline Company so I found a job with the Peterborough branch of National Grocers. They were expanding and needed a couple of truck drivers.

Since I was an experienced truck driver, thanks to my father, they gave me a forty-five foot tractor-trailer to drive. It was a good job. I hauled a lot of frozen foods including French fries. Here I was back in the frozen potato business.

Being an entrepreneur, I decided to install a few swimming pools part time. I had done work on a few pools in the Toronto area when we lived there.

The first pool I installed was for a real estate man who had just started his own company. He said that if I would refer business to him he promised to steer swimming pool jobs in my direction.

The rest is history. I became so busy I had to reluctantly leave my job at National Grocers.

Now that I was owner of a company I was excited, but the company had no name. After considerable debate with my wife, and through a process of elimination, we came up with the title "Peterborough Pool and Patio" or PPP.

These were uncharted waters and there were times when I wondered if this business was the right decision. I would work on the job all day and about five p.m. we would load our two kids in my van with some blankets so they could sleep. We would take off to Toronto to pick up a pool kit after making arrangements to meet the shipper late at night. We often got home at two a.m.

Sunday was just another workday for us. We now had a crew of men and they were working sixty and seventy hours a week.

After spending a couple of summers in the pool business we ended up with a bank account, a situation to which I was unaccustomed.

RUST NEVER SLEEPS

I received a phone call from a customer whose pool filter was leaking and went to look at it. I discovered a filter tank, at least twenty years old, with rust holes in its sides.

I looked at that huge tank, which must have weighed a thousand pounds, and decided that I didn't want to remove it to install a new one.

To repair it, I drilled out the rust holes and inserted a wood plug in each hole. The plugs absorbed water and sealed the leaks. It worked great. I told Scott that his pool filter was good for one more year.

The next year I had to go back and plug some new holes. Each year I would tell Scott that the pool was good for one more year. This went on for about four years, prompting Scott to say that he should write a book about me doctoring up his filter every year.

Finally, the inevitable happened. We had to remove the filter. It looked like a porcupine with the wood plugs protruding all over the surface.

I recruited some good, strong men. With a great deal of pushing and shoving we finally got the monstrosity out of the basement.

There was an old truck, which belonged to his son, sitting in the yard. Scribbled on the rear bumper were the words: "Rust Never Sleeps." Scott directed us to roll the filter onto the truck.

The above-mentioned Scott was, and still is, Scott Young of literary fame. The old truck belonged to his son, Neil Young, and the rusty old filter tank bore testimonial to the song title on his bumper.

To learn more about this famous family, I advise you to purchase the literary masterpiece *Neil and Me*. I give you fair warning—you may not be able to put the book down.

FAMILY VACATIONS

The summers had been so hectic that we had had little time for vacations and the brief trips we made only served to whet our appetite for travel. We decided it was time to indulge this appetite. We loaded the kids in the van and headed for Florida.

It was March Break so the kids were out of school. It was springtime, and it was like old times being on the road again.

That was the year of the Big Frost in Florida. It froze almost every night and all of the plants and flowers were drooping. It killed over half of all the orange trees in Florida.

We took the kids to Florida, Myrtle Beach, or somewhere warm for a week or two every year after that until they were finished high school. On several occasions when they were in high school, they would each bring a friend. We had a lot of fun and good times on these holidays with the kids.

Since then we have gone somewhere almost every winter. We have been to Mexico and Colombia. We have taken cruises, and been to many of the Caribbean Islands and southern states.

When Pam was about eleven years old we headed for Florida and she became ill not far into the trip. We had reserved a place on Sanibel Island for two weeks and after we were there a few days she became seriously ill. We got the ambulance to take her to the hospital in Fort Myers.

We left Sanibel Island and rented a motel close to the hospital in Fort Myers where we stayed for almost a week before she was released. This was one week we spent in Florida that was not much fun.

When she was released from the hospital, we headed for home immediately. We still remember our holiday on Sanibel Island.

HOCKEY WITH THE KIDS

When Bryan was five years old he wanted to play hockey so we enrolled him in the tyke level of the Church hockey league in Peterborough. He was a terrible skater and not aggressive like some of the other kids. I let him struggle through the season and decided that was probably the end of hockey around our house.

The following year the same Church League team needed a goalie, so the coach phoned me and asked if we would let Bryan play goal. Against my better judgment I agreed. The coach worked with him and I began to see signs of improvement.

The following year I became coach of the Church League team and we had a good year. Bryan was beginning to look like a goalie.

The following year I was asked to coach an atom team in the PMHA, which was the other house league in Peterborough. It was more competitive than the Church League so I accepted the coaching job.

Bryan came along to play for me in the PMHA. About two games into the season I got a phone call one evening telling me that the new coach who took my place on last year's team had had a heart attack.

A voice on the phone said: "Ivan would you please coach the team until we find a new coach?" I guess it was because the guy said "please," but anyway I accepted. I was now coaching two atom hockey teams.

About this time the Girl's Hockey league was almost ready to start. A couple of Pam's friends were hockey players and they asked her if she wanted to play. Pam came to me and asked if I would coach the girls' team. Now I was coaching three teams. I was at the rink almost every night and it created more than a few problems at home.

Sue was getting a little ticked off—for good reason. If I was home one night each week I was lucky. I had three games per week and three practice sessions. I was a rink rat!

The Church League team looked rather hopeless at the beginning of the season but they improved with every game. I coached them to the championship finals where they lost by one goal. Those kids were like family that winter. I was very proud of them.

I coached Bryan's team in the City League to the finals, although they also lost out. They too were great kids and I was proud to be their coach.

Pam had enough of hockey around mid-season. She left the team and I was rather glad she did. Pam was a young lady now and the rowdy game of hockey was not for her. That was the last year that I coached hockey.

HOCKEY WITH THE ALL STARS

Bryan began playing all-star hockey in Ennismore, a village where he went to public school. He began playing at the peewee level and we went to tournaments all over Ontario, which helped to pass the winter months.

The Ennismore Pee Wees was a super team. They were in the All Ontario finals four years in a row, which meant they were still playing hockey in May. This interfered somewhat with our pool business, which is always busy in May.

The tournaments were exciting. Bryan was improving as a goalie and I began to hold practices at home with him. The Ennismore team won all of their league games. They went to the All Ontario Finals and lost out in the final game, but the next year the team won the All Ontario Championship.

I decided to enroll Bryan in hockey school in the summer. He was in seventh heaven because NHL stars were the instructors, including Bobby Carpenter, Paul Coffey, Greg Millen and later on Gordie Howe.

When the sessions were over the pros would put on their skates and skate with the kids. Once I went to pick Bryan up at the end of a day and he was still on the ice playing with the pros. Bryan, being a goalie always felt good if he stopped a shot from one of these guys. One time Paul Coffey came barreling down the ice. He was amazingly fast. He put the puck in the net and took it out and Bryan didn't even know it had gone in. It was so fast that I didn't see it and I was close by.

A couple of years later the Ennismore team won the All Ontario Championship for the second time. Bryan was chosen as the star of the game. He now had two All Ontario Championships. Few minor hockey players ever receive even one All Ontario Championship ring.

We saw a lot of hockey and it made the winters enjoyable and exciting. Bryan played on the school team all the time he was in high school, and when he left to go to the University of Western Ontario in London we missed the hockey in the winter. Bryan played for a junior C team from Lucan while he was at Western.

We would have liked to see this team play but the mileage factor was against us.

OUR DREAM HOME

Things were going quite well in the swimming pool business so we decided to build our dream home.

We found a beautiful wooded lot in the suburbs. At this time we also purchased plans for our dream house. It was now time to put a "For Sale" sign on our house in Fairbairn Meadows.

We worked at the pool business until about five o'clock in the evening. With the aid of a yard light we worked on the new house until about midnight each day. The kids were young and slept on beds in the van while we worked. Since this was summer, they didn't have to go to school the next day.

At last the house was finished. It was a beautiful house and we lived there for about seven years. After all these years every time we drive by that house I still take pride in the fact that we built it almost entirely by ourselves.

We sold our home and bought a new house in Peterborough. With our kids soon to be gone we didn't need a large house, and we felt more at ease leaving Pam alone here in town.

It was 1990 and we were suddenly in a recession, and very few people were having swimming pools installed.

I spent a couple of summers in Toronto with my truck and excavator because I had very little work in Peterborough. I dug pools for larger companies in the Toronto area.

A short time later the economy improved and I was busy again in Peterborough. Now came a bit of bad timing on our part. We opened a branch in Cobourg.

As well as swimming pools, we were selling water softeners, bottled water, high efficiency stoves etc. This was a colossal mistake and after we closed it down it took us many years to pay off the debt.

Since we lived in the Beautiful Kawarthas we decided to buy a boat and do some boating. Another mistake! We had little time for a boat. The boating season conflicts with our work season, which almost totally consumes any leisure time in the summer.

We did some snowmobiling for a few winters in the seventies. We would go almost every weekend all winter with two other couples and their families. We had a great time and each Sunday we took turns making dinner for the gang.

I still get itchy feet in the spring. I guess the "spring fever" thing will follow me for the rest of my life.

Our lifestyle is certainly unique, either feast or famine. Summertime is dawn until dusk at work and wintertime is dawn until dusk doing almost nothing, except for the winters when the kids played hockey and other sports etc.

I often reminisce about the life I once had, the old gang, the jobs in new and strange places. Such is life!

Pam upon graduation from Lakehead University.

Bryan upon graduation from Western University.

A DAUGHTER EXTRAORDINARY

Pam was, by now, enrolled at Sir Sandford Fleming College in Peterborough. On Friday, December thirteenth, Pam was in a car accident. Does December thirteenth, ring a bell? My birthday!

Pam injured one knee and it required surgery. This meant that she missed a lot of classes and hobbled around on crutches for many more classes. In spite of all these adversities, through Pam's determination, she graduated on the Dean's list.

I will never forget the day she walked up to the front, fresh off her crutches, to receive her diploma. When I remembered what she went through that year to get to this point I was overwhelmed with emotion. I was proud to have such a fine daughter.

Pam won a scholarship from Human Resources Professional Association of Ontario. She enrolled in Lakehead University in Thunder Bay to further her education. She left for Lakehead on crutches and it was another emotional time.

During Pam's year at Lakehead her mother and I had our twenty-fifth wedding anniversary. We had planned a Caribbean cruise and we were scheduled to leave on Saturday night for an early flight Sunday morning to Miami to board the cruise ship.

Pam came home from Lakehead University that weekend and informed us that she was taking us out to dinner to celebrate our anniversary before we went on the cruise.

We ended up at one of the fine dining places in the Peterborough area. When we walked through the door we were flabbergasted. About forty of our friends and relatives were there, some from quite a distance away.

When we caught our breath I began to wonder how we were going to get to the airport on time. Pam told us not to worry. A limousine had been arranged to take us to the airport and our hotel reservation had been cancelled.

When we arrived in Miami and boarded the ship there was a beautiful flower arrangement in our cabin with a tag that said "Happy Anniversary." Pam had arranged almost all of this from Thunder Bay, a distance of nearly eight hundred miles away.

Later that year we flew to Thunder Bay to attend Pam's graduation from Lakehead University. Proudly we watched Pam go to the podium for yet another diploma.

The following year we drove to London to attend Bryan's graduation from Western University. It was another special occasion.

Anyone who has attended a son or daughter's graduation will agree with me when I say that it's a very special and proud experience.

LIFE WITH TWO WOMEN

Pam being a young lady now meant that I had two women in my life. I had barely gotten accustomed to the priorities of one woman and along comes woman number two.

They tried to teach me a lot of important things, like how to peel a banana from the right end. My wife Sue has a phobia about dirty car windows and my truck windows sometimes get pretty grubby. Enter Sue with the window wand. Sue also has a phobia about slippery roads and sidewalks.

They tried to teach me that I must not leave the house unless my clothes are "colour coordinated" a rule that has met with more than a few problems since I am slightly colour-blind.

Thirty-five years and I'm still not sure which side of the plate to put the knife and fork and I still forget to put the toilet seat down. You just can't teach an old dog new tricks. Someone once said, "Men are from Mars, women are from Venus." In my opinion they are farther apart than that.

Almost all of my life I have been surrounded by male friends. I was raised as one of five brothers. Our village was almost all boys in my growing years. The path that I chose in life on construction left me in a rough and rowdy environment. A great part of my life was spent on the seat of an excavator or listening to vulgar stories in the bunkhouse. It tends to make me a little rough around the edges.

Pam and Sue's project of trying to smooth out these rough edges has come to be, in all probability, an exercise in futility.

When I was a young whipper-snapper on the QNS job, an old timer took me under his wing and proceeded to tell me about the real world: "Keep your eyes and ears open and your mouth shut, and don't ask questions." He explained: "If you ask questions, people will judge your level of intelligence by the questions you ask. Nine times out of ten they will deliberately give you a wrong answer. If you follow these simple rules," he said, "you can probably end up as smart as the average lawyer or teacher."

It seems I didn't adhere to his words of wisdom entirely because I don't think I want to compete with a lawyer or teacher. Besides I am still learning.

GIVING OUR DAUGHTER AWAY

The day I walked Pam down the aisle to the altar was a very special and emotional moment. She is married to a really super guy. The wedding was beautiful but, alas, I missed a lot of the reception. You just can't see much looking through the bottom of a Danish Schnapps glass.

Pam and Peter live in a beautiful house in Georgetown, Ontario, and Pam worked as a human resources manager for a large company in Brampton until she and Peter started a family. They now have three sons. I guess like all grandparents we spoil our grandsons, and love every minute we can spend together.

WEDDING NUMBER TWO

Two weeks after I walked Pam down the aisle I had the honour of walking another little girl down the aisle to her wedding.

Her father had passed away a few years before and I assumed the role of father or at least guardian.

I felt very proud to be included in her wedding and thoroughly approved her choice of husband. She too married a really great man. They have, at this point, three daughters who also like to call me grandpa.

OUR SON LEAVES HOME

Bryan has an executive job in Atlanta, Georgia. We went to New Jersey to attend another beautiful wedding when Bryan married a lovely girl named Susan.

I feel that both Pam and Bryan made excellent choices of a spouse. Of course I firmly believe that they inherited this trait from their father.

Springtime is still my favourite season. The whole world comes alive after the long winter. That also is the season when I come back to life. We make maple syrup on a small scale and listen to the birds singing. This is usually when my spring fever kicks in.

Just before we open the pool business for the summer we like to throw a suitcase in the car and head south. Not the suitcase of my younger days! It has long since gone the way of the dodo bird, besides we now need room for two people's belongings.

TIME OUT

Through thirty years in the pool business we have acquired an experienced staff. They are capable of operating the business so we take a week or two off each summer. With our camper and canoe we head up to the Algonquin Park area to do some camping. There is a beautiful canoe lake just inside the park border at Petawawa. We like to go canoeing and fishing on this lake and watch the otters at play.

The call of the loon as he hunts for fish is one of the great sounds of the backwoods.

Our backyard on Mountland Drive, Peterborough

REMINISCING

As a kid in public school I heard about far away places, but never in my wildest dreams did I expect to see any of them.

As I sit back and reminisce I suddenly realize that I have been to most of them and more: Labrador, Moosonee, Churchill, the Northwest

Our boat, a 22 foot Bayliner, in Bobcaygeon.

Territories, the Yukon and the Rockies. I have seen life as it was in the gold rush days. As well, I have been in all ten provinces of Canada.

In the USA I have been in many states. I have visited Florida often and travelled to Georgia, the Virginias, Michigan and south to Arkansas, Mississippi, and Louisiana. I have been to the great state of Texas with its romantic cities–historic Galveston, San Antonio, the Alamo, and Dallas where I had my picture taken standing on the bronze marker where John F. Kennedy was shot to death.

I have been through the hill country in Texas to Lyndon Johnson's estate and seen his grave under an oak tree on the LBJ Ranch. I also visited Andrew Jackson's grave on the Jackson estate.

In Arlington Cemetery I solemnly stood in front of the eternal flame on the grave of JFK. Brother Bobby Kennedy's grave is close by. Robert E. Lee is buried here as well.

In the great state of Tennessee we visited a lookout in Rock City where it is possible to see seven states. We have been to the Grand Ol' Opry in Nashville. We visited Memphis and had a ride on a Mississippi river boat.

One should never go to Memphis without visiting Graceland mansion where Elvis Presley lived and died. The huge garage

170

housed Elvis' seven Cadillacs. Elvis is buried beside his mother in the meditation garden of the estate.

In North Carolina Biltmore Estate is, in my opinion, one of the wonders of the world.

We have seen the awesome sights of Las Vegas, the beautiful Nevada Desert, and Hoover Dam, an amazing man-made marvel. We have travelled through Death Valley and the Mojave Desert of California.

We were able to visit Matamoros Mexico where we witnessed unspeakable poverty. A different and more affluent part of Mexico is on the west coast. Puerto Vallarta is a beautiful area to spend a winter holiday and go whale watching.

We have been to Costa Rica and through the Panama Canal. We visited the primitive San Blas Islands of Panama, where the Cuna Indians live the same lifestyle that they have lived for centuries.

Santa Marta and the ancient city of Cartagena, Colombia, were interesting places. We have been high in the Andes Mountains of Colombia where coffee is grown. This altitude is also where the cocaine industry is thriving.

I have spent time on many of the Caribbean Islands.

I visited many of the Bahama Islands when I was working on Grand Bahama: Bimini, Nassau, primitive Mayaguana, and San Salvador where Columbus allegedly first landed when he discovered the New World in fourteen ninety-two.

In Dominican Republic we toured the church in Santo Domingo where the ashes of Columbus are in an urn at the front of the church. The church is over four hundred years old and has withstood many terrible storms over the centuries. It is the oldest church in the New World.

Barbados, Trinidad and Tobago were interesting islands. While in Tobago we experienced a huge tidal wave, which was powerful enough to injure some of the beachcombers.

I have not made it to the other side of the Atlantic, although it is in our future plans.

In the Americas we have the beautiful, the barren, the cold, the hot, the hilly, and the prairies, each with a beauty of its own.

I am sure that I have forgotten some of the places that I have been but I think, rather than subject the reader to further boredom, I will say that I am at home in Peterborough, Ontario.

I like to do a little armchair travelling in the winter but in the springtime we like to do the real thing, so we usually head south for a week or two to shake off the winter blahs.

Along with my love of travel it seems that three of my favourite things are fast cars, beautiful women and Dutch apple pie. Perhaps it should read beautiful cars, fast women and Dutch apple pie.

Whatever way you take it, it seems that everything I like is illegal, immoral, or fattening.

BETTER TO GIVE

There is one more thing that rates high on my list. That is the old saying, "It is better to give than to receive." I enjoy helping people and I find there are many people in the world that can use a little help.

As a Lions Club member I come face to face with many people in need.

One example was a lady in Lindsay, Ontario. She had lost a leg due to complications but she loved to swim. Our Company installed a backyard pool for her but she had problems getting in and out of it so I built a derrick with a winch. A cable was installed to a special chair. She got out of her wheelchair into the pool chair and the winch picked the pool chair up and swung it over the water. We then lowered the chair into the water. She would get off and after paddling around in the pool she would get back in the chair and her husband hoisted her up on the pool deck. The look of gratitude that I received was worth it all and more.

Another time a couple contracted to have a new pool installed by our Company. I delivered the components and they paid me a down payment.

A few days later I received a phone call from the lady telling me that she and her husband had separated. I went to her place and loaded up all the pool components and refunded every cent of her payment. She put her head on my shoulder and cried she was so happy. She didn't say anything. She didn't have to.

We put a pool in for another lady many years ago and have been back occasionally to do maintenance etc. Her husband left her shortly after we installed the pool, so money was a problem for her, as she had three young children to raise.

In later years while we were doing repairs to the pool she remarked that one of her dreams was to have a roof on her backyard patio but she just didn't have the money to have it done.

I passed it off and about four years later she mentioned it again. I decided, hey, I could do this job and save her a lot of money, so I rebuilt the deck. The lady stood back in her yard looking at the deck as if she saw a miracle. All she could say was: "It's beautiful. It's beautiful. I can't believe it."

MATURITY SETS IN

Since December of 1932 a lot of water and some whiskey has gone under the bridge. I have grown long in the tooth and short in the memory. My eyes and ears are running about half throttle which, I find isn't all bad. I have seen more places and sights than I ever dreamed possible. There are some things such as alarm clocks that I don't miss hearing.

I am beginning to like the senior discounts at the corner store. I even had one lady tell me that I looked too young to collect senior discounts. I gave her a nice tip.

In the summer I still go into the shop and stir things up and get in the way. I don't think I will ever stop work.

My entire working life has been spent in the construction of highways, railroads, airports and more. The past thirty years I have been in swimming pool construction. One can't do this type of work for this many years without acquiring considerable knowledge on the subject.

I am happy to pass this knowledge on to my customers and also my employees. I learned it by trial and error but I can pass it on to them straight from the horse's mouth. Facts and figures are really not my thing. I am a nuts and bolts person—meaning I came up through the trenches.

I have experienced failure and I have experienced success and the success came mainly because I learned from my failures.

I was never a politician, a doctor or a lawyer, or as you have probably noticed by now a writer.

In my own way I have striven to be the best at my profession and I hope I will leave this world a little better than I found it.

In grade nine of High School I learned a poem that has stuck with me through the years. It goes something like this:

BE THE BEST OF WHATEVER YOU ARE

If you can't be the pine at the top of the hill
Be a scrub in the valley, but be
The best little scrub by the side of the rill
Be a bush if you can't be a tree
If a train you can't be, be the rail
If you can't be the moon, be a star
It isn't by size that you win or you fail
Be the best of whatever you are!

CPSIA information can be obtained
at www.ICGtesting.com
Printed in the USA
BVHW070735081021
618386BV00001B/47

9 781412 018227